ARTHUR LISTON

the
choice
is yours

A BOOK OF SERMONS

EPWORTH PRESS

© Arthur R. Liston 1972
First published 1972
by the Epworth Press
All Rights Reserved
No part of this publication
may be reproduced, stored in a
retrieval system, or
transmitted, in any form or by
any means, electronic, mechanical,
photocopying, recording or
otherwise, without the prior
permission of the Epworth Press,
27 Marylebone Road, London NW1 5JS
Printed and bound in
Great Britain by
The Garden City Press Limited,
Letchworth, Hertfordshire SG6 1JS

SBN 7162 0209 3

Enquiries should be addressed to
The Distributors
The Methodist Book Room
2 Chester House, Pages Lane
Muswell Hill, London N10 1PZ

Contents

To my wife
IRENE

ONE

A Bunch of Everlastings

'I have loved thee with an everlasting love'   Jeremiah 31, verse 3

Whenever I think of Salzburg, that lovely old Austrian town which away back in 1756 was Mozart's birthplace, I find myself wandering around its ancient narrow streets, in particular looking at the beautiful bunches of multicoloured dried flowers which seem to be on sale in nearly every other shop, and especially from stalls which ornament the squares of that particularly charming town.

When we were there we talked about buying a bunch of such 'everlastings'. In the end, however, we decided not to do so. Quite apart from the fact that they were so expensive, we really had no confidence that they would stand up to being transferred from one European camping site to another. In other words, 'everlastings' though they were called, we had doubts about their being able, as it were, 'to last' till we got home!

On this first Sunday of 1971 I want to present you with what might aptly, and I hope not too mawkishly, be described as a 'bunch of everlastings' which during the past week I have gathered from the pages of the Bible in general —and (as it turned out) from the pages of the Old Testament in particular.

It is my hope that this little bunch—actually it's more like a posy—of colourful 'everlastings' will be treasured by you, and turn out to be valuable to you, especially in the course of any drab and dreary, not to say disturbing and distressing, days which may be before you during the New Year.

It was the third verse in Jeremiah chapter 31 which started me out on my search for Biblical 'everlastings'— 'I have loved thee with an everlasting love.'

But no sooner had I set out on my quest for Scriptural 'everlastings' than my arms were filled with magnificent blooms, or to speak more prosaically, my sheets of paper were covered with superb references, many of which seemed to be crying out for inclusion in this morning's New Year Presentation Bunch.

So I had to get down to the task of selection and arrangement, to deciding which everlastings we should talk about today and especially to deciding how we should talk about them.

It didn't take me long to decide that I needn't include in my 'bunch of everlastings' any allusion to 'everlasting hills' or even to 'everlasting mountains'. You see, in spite of the fact that there are several such Biblical references—even the hills, even the mountains these days cannot be regarded as being 'everlasting'. Just the other evening on television I saw a Russian hill being turned into a valley by means of an underground nuclear explosion.

On the other hand, I had to ponder long over a whole wide range of other 'everlastings' which seem to grow in considerable profusion on the pages of Scripture. In the end, however, I realized that for our purposes on this first Sunday of 1971—and especially for our benefit throughout all of 1971—'everlasting' references directly to the Lord our God were of the greatest significance.

So it is that we begin with a simple, straightforward reference to

THE EVERLASTING GOD.

As you might expect, there are several such references in Scripture. Probably the best known is to be found in Isaiah chapter 40 and verse 8—'Hast thou not known? Hast thou not heard that *the everlasting God*, the Lord, the Creator of the ends of the earth, fainteth not, neither is weary?'

The Hebrews were always at pains to emphasize the 'everlastingness' of their God. They called Him *Elohim*—'The powerful one who is eternal', or again, they called Him *Jahweh*—'I am'—'I am that I am'. And Christian people have followed the Hebrew example, referring to their Lord as 'The Alpha and Omega'—'The beginning and the ending'—'The one which was and is and is yet to come'—'The same yesterday and today and for ever'.

Not for the Jews or the Christians a God who dies out, or ever gets tired out. Their Lord is

'an everlasting God—one who fainteth not neither is weary'.

These days it's none too easy to put your finger on lasting things—on long-lasting—let alone on everlasting things. Time was, not so very long ago, when from one year to another things didn't change all that much. These days nothing seems to last all that long. Fashions and fads, modes, manners, and even moralities, all seem to change with bewildering rapidity. If, after a few years, you revisit a town which once you knew well, the chances are that you'll hardly recognize it. Allow a few years to pass, and then visit a bit of country which you once knew and loved well, and yet again the chances are that you'll hardly recognize it.

When my parents moved to their present home, from the front bedroom window there was a fine distant view of the Drumchapel hills—in winter often covered with snow and during the summer often bathed in sunlight. The last time I visited them, I noticed that the beauty of those hills had been utterly destroyed, for the Drumchapel Hills had been almost entirely covered with the Drumchapel estate! 'Everlasting hills' indeed! Nowadays you don't even need a nuclear explosion to destroy such things of beauty.

And, of course, just as places change, so do people! From

7

my reading, and especially from my contact with elderly folk, I conclude that but a few years ago people seemed to change little, if at all, from year to year. So much so that it was often possible for a man to leave his home town for quite a period of time and then to return to it and take up life again, and especially take up relationships again, as though there had been no interruption. Could you imagine that happening today? Of course not, for in this era of rapid change, people change even more rapidly than places. So much so that the homesick exile who for years has longed to be back in his native land, amongst his 'ain folk', is likely to be sadly dis-appointed, may be even bitterly disillusioned when at last he makes the return journey. It's not just that places change so rapidly these days. So do people.

A month or so ago I found myself in conversation with a fellow Scot, a fellow Glaswegian indeed, who is now within sight of retirement. 'Are you going back to Glasgow when you retire?' I asked him. 'Not on your life!' was his immediate reply. Then he told me of a recent visit to the city which in his childhood, youth and young manhood he had dearly loved. 'You know,' he said, 'when I walked the streets of Glasgow, and especially when I called in at the homes of one-time Glasgow friends, I felt like a visitor from another planet.'

Certainly we live in an era of rapid change. These days few things seem to last long—sad to say—not even one-time close relationships. In such an era we need to have knowledge of—

and especially contact with one who 'changes not'—
with one who is long-lasting;
if possible,
with one who is everlasting.

In the last analysis, there is none other who merits such a description than He who—as the Psalmist puts it—

is 'from everlasting to everlasting'.

So with confidence, this first Sunday in a New Year, I refer

you to
    the God and Father of our Lord Jesus Christ,
       that is, of course,
          to *the everlasting God.*

But this 'everlasting God' and Father of our Lord Jesus Christ is also
      AN EVER LOVING GOD.

More than once over Christmas, we've listened to the words of Isaiah the Old Testament prophet—
'For unto us a child is born, unto us a son is given, and the government shall be upon his shoulder, and his name shall be called, wonderful counsellor, the mighty God, *the everlasting Father,* the Prince of Peace.'

'The everlasting Father.' A clear reference to the precious truth that the everlasting God we worship is also an ever loving God.

But of course we don't need any such oblique reference to the everlasting love of our God. In Jeremiah chapter 31 and verse 3 we have a direct reference to it. 'I have loved thee', says the Almighty through His prophet Jeremiah, 'with an everlasting love.'

A man can put up with all sorts of changes around him so long as his 'loved ones' don't change towards him.

Surely it was this very point that Principal Rainey was making when, in explaining to a friend who met him on Princes Street, Edinburgh how he managed to remain carefree in the midst of so much calumny and insult, he said, 'Man, I'm happy at home!'

In other words, 'I don't care how many of my fellows hate me, or even how much they hate me, so long as I'm loved by my loved ones.'

But in these days when so many marriages are breaking down and so many homes are breaking up, a great many people are discovering to their distress that they are not really

9

and truly loved even by their loved ones.

But at this point in a year during which at least one person in this Church is bound to discover that he's not loved as once he was, or even as he still thought he was, not even by his loved ones, what can I helpfully do?

Nothing more and nothing better than draw attention yet again to the everlasting love of the everlasting God and assure you that even if nobody loves you, and even if nobody else has any great cause to love you—God does!

'Can a woman's tender care
Cease towards the child she bare?
Yes, she may forgetful be;
Yet will I remember thee.'

'I have loved thee—and I will love thee—with an everlasting love.'

So our everlasting God is an ever loving God.

Allow me now to add that He's also
AN EVER LISTENING GOD.

That verse from Isaiah chapter 40 comes back to mind—the one about 'the everlasting God who fainteth not neither is weary'. Thinking along the same lines the Psalmist refers to his God as the one who 'neither slumbers nor sleeps'.

With those words before us, I would now submit that our everlasting, ever loving God is also an ever listening God.

I don't know about you, but I draw a good deal of consolation from this thought. No matter when I call my heavenly Father up in prayer, He's never too busy to listen to me. And more than that, no matter how often I call my heavenly Father up in prayer, even if it be to make the same old request that I've made a thousand times before, the same request for pardon, the same request for power, He's never too busy—or too bored—to listen to me. Though He be night and day at the receiving end of my prayer, my everlasting, ever loving God never gets faint or grows weary, He never, ever, 'slumbers or sleeps'. He is an ever listening God.

But in the few moments that remain to me there's just one more 'everlasting' which I would want to add to the bunch, and which I would have you carry away with you this day—and always carry with you through the days of the coming year. It is to be found in Deuteronomy chapter 33 and verse 27.
'The eternal God is thy refuge and underneath are the everlasting arms.'
And just because there's little point in talking about everlastings which don't even linger in the memory, I would now invite you to think with me for a few moments about

OUR EVER LEADING GOD

the one who always guides His people with love.
In this reference to the everlasting arms, you see, I discover an assurance not only that God 'holds His people up' but that He also 'leads His people on'.
Our everlasting, ever loving, ever listening God is also an ever leading God. And as I stand on the threshold of a mysterious year, I say 'Thank God' for the everlasting, ever leading arms.
'I said to the man who stood at the gate of the year, "Give me a light that I may tread safely into the unknown." And he replied, "Go out into the darkness and put your hand into the hand of God. That shall be to you better than a light and safer than a known way." '
The everlasting hand,
     the everlasting arm of God
          which guides us out into the unknown.

So for 1971 I have much pleasure in presenting to you

a fine little bunch of everlastings. And just in case you're inclined to let one or other of them fall as you leave church and head for home this morning, I would firmly tie them all together for you yet again, and send you away thinking gladly, especially gratefully about your everlasting,

ever loving,

ever listening,

and ever leading God.

TWO

The Mind of Christ

Declares the Apostle Paul, with quite staggering confidence, in his first letter to the Corinthians, chapter 2, and verse 16—
'*We possess the mind of Christ.*'

Dr Moffatt in his translation of the New Testament brings out even more vividly the staggeringly confident element in the Apostolic declaration. He renders it—
'Our thoughts are Christ's thoughts.'

Confronted by this quite remarkable claim, anybody who has an even passing familiarity with the Old Testament immediately finds himself thinking of a couple of verses which occur in Isaiah, chapter 55.
'My thoughts are not your thoughts, neither are your ways my ways, saith the Lord. For as the heavens are higher than the earth, so are my ways higher than your ways and my thoughts than your thoughts.'

Was the Apostle Paul ignorant of, or had he forgotten about these words when he confidently declared—'Our thoughts are Christ's thoughts'? Apparently not, for just before making this stupendous claim Paul actually quotes the prophet Isaiah. In effect Paul says something like this:
'Isaiah the prophet demands,
"Who knows the mind of the Lord? Who can understand the thoughts of the Lord?"
Well,' Paul goes on confidently, 'we Christians have the answer to Isaiah's question, for we possess the mind of Christ.'

Confronted by those words, two questions come at once to

my mind. First of all—*how did Christ think*?
What sort of things did Jesus Christ the child,
    the boy,
        the youth and the man,
—what sort of things did He think about? In what way did
He think about them?

Not so very surprisingly this is a question which again and
again I found myself asking when I visited the Holy Land,
and especially when for a week I lived just outside Nazareth.

My hotel was magnificently sited on the hills immediately
to the south overlooking Nazareth. My bedroom window
looked out towards the so-called Mount of Precipitation,
possibly the very 'steep place' to which the citizens of Nazareth
dragged our Lord with murderous intent.

Often of a morning, quite early, once or twice just as the
sun was rising, I got up and looked over the Nazareth Hills,
towards the Mount of Precipitation. As I stood there with
only the crowing of cocks and the barking of dogs to break
the silence, I found myself thinking :
'Early in the morning Jesus must often have climbed up into
those very hills.
Perhaps as a man,
    as a youth,
        and even as a boy,
He came here for solitude and stillness,
    may be to pray,
        and may be just to think.
What sort of things did He think about? In what way did He
think about them?'

While we were at Nazareth the Jewish Passover was
celebrated and our Israeli hosts invited us to share their
Passover meal—an experience which none of us who were
there can ever forget.

Immediately following the passover meal, some of us went

14

out for an evening stroll. In the brilliance of the full passover
moon, we walked along the hill road above Nazareth. As we
walked it occurred to us that possibly Jesus the boy, the
youth, the man, following one or more such Passover Meal,
feeling deeply,
    as He was bound to feel,
        the religious significance of the Passover,
possibly He made His way up into those very moonlit hills,
    to pray,
        or just to think.
But up in the hills, lit by the full moon of Passover,
    how did Jesus think?
What sort of things did He think about? How did He think
about them?

Now obviously, up in the hills above Nazareth and down
in Nazareth itself, our Lord's thoughts must have been legion.
He must have thought about His home and His business,
about His family and His friends,
about His responsibilities and about His recreation,
and so on.
But surely above and beyond all else,
He must have thought about His identity and His destiny.

He must often have thought about His I D E N T I T Y.

At Christmas time we think a good deal about what the
theologians call 'The Incarnation', about the fact that in the
person of Jesus Christ, who was born at Bethlehem and who
lived most of His life in Nazareth, God became man. 'God
was in Christ.'
    But at what point in His life did our Lord become conscious
of this fact? One of the Apocryphal Gospels fancifully suggests
that this was an awareness which our Lord had from birth,
and that the baby Jesus one day sat bolt upright and told
His mother plainly, 'I am the Son of God.'

Surely never! Surely this was a gradual awareness that dawned on our Lord
as He played with other children,
as He grew up with other adolescents,
and as He worked with the other men in Nazareth,
and especially, as a boy, a youth, and a man,
He wandered over the hills above His little home town.
Gradually, He must have become aware of the fact
that though He was like other children, youth and men,
He was remarkably unlike them.
'Who am I?' He must repeatedly have asked Himself.
Then slowly,
   but at the same time relentlessly,
      the answer to His own question must have dawned on
      Him.
'Son of Mary though I am, I am also the Son of God.'

Our Lord must often have thought about His *identity*.

   But having established His identity,
      He must often have gone on to ponder His D E S T I N Y.
'Who am I?'
'I am the Son of God.'
'But what am I here for? What have I come to do?'

No doubt, as He thought about His destiny, our Lord
began to realize that within the world He had a double
purpose. He had 'to reveal God to men' and
He had 'to reconcile men to God'.
What did our Lord think about?
He must often have thought about His identity and about
His destiny.

   But an equally important question to ask is—
'In what way did our Lord think about His identity and

about His destiny?'
He could, of course, have thought about both *proudly*,
and then gone on to speak about both quite arrogantly.
Wouldn't His brothers,

   His sisters,

     His neighbours and His customers
be surprised if they were to learn that He was none other
than the Son of God, born into the world

  so that He might reveal God to men,

     and reconcile men to God?
Like His humble little mother, however, our Lord,
'kept all these things and pondered them in His heart',
at least until the day came for Him to leave Nazareth and
begin His Ministry.

Our Lord thought much about His identity

   and about His destiny.

     But He thought about both with H U M I L I T Y.
That's how our Lord thought!

   Apparently, we as Christians *can* think as our Lord thought.
At least this is the confident claim made by the Apostle Paul.
'We possess the mind of Christ.'
'Our thoughts are Christ's thoughts.'
Like our Lord before us,

  we can,

    and we must

      think about our I D E N T I T Y.
and, of course, as Christians,

  we have a very remarkable identity.
We are the children of God,

  men and women who through faith in Jesus Christ
have entered into a very special and highly intimate relationship with God Almighty Himself.
He came unto His own and His own received Him not.

But as many as received Him, to them He gave the power to become the sons of God, even to them that believe on His name.'

The Christian is a child of God.
That's his true identity and he should often think about his identity.

The trouble with most of us is that we don't think enough about our true identity.
Just because we look like,
and have to work,
eat and sleep like those who are no more than 'sons of men',
we ourselves tend rather to shelve the thought that we,
    through faith in Jesus Christ,
       are truly the Sons and Daughters of God.

And, of course, because we fail to think sufficiently
       about our true identity,
    we tend to forget our true D E S T I N Y. as Christian people.
You see, like our Lord before us,
    it is our destiny to reveal God to men,
       and even to reconcile men to their God.
Certainly it is our destiny to reveal God to men.

    This is how the Apostle Paul makes this very point in the course of his second Epistle to the Corinthians.
'You are a letter that has come from Christ,
a letter written not with ink,
but with the Spirit of the living God,
written not on stone tables,
but on the pages of the human heart.'
With equal force the Apostle Paul might simply have said

to the Corinthians,
'It is your destiny as Christians to reveal God to men.'

But it is also the destiny of the Christian to reconcile men to
God.
'God was in Christ reconciling the world to Himself.'
Yes,
    but more than that,
        'God has entrusted us with the message of
        reconciliation'—
           a message which we must preach with our lips
            and illustrate with our lives.
We Christians, like our Lord before us,
    must think much about our identity.
        and about our destiny.

But again, like our Lord before us,
    We must think about both with H U M I L I T Y.
    The New Testament is full of warnings against pride,
and especially against spiritual pride,
    the pride that tragically can develop in the heart of the
    Christian
        who thinks much about his remarkable identity and
        destiny.
In particular, the New Testament is full of exhortations to
humility, especially to spiritual humility,
    to what in one place is described as 'humbleness of mind'
    (Colossians 3 : 12).
And, of course, the greatest of such exhortations is to be
discovered in Philippians, chapter 2.
'Let this mind be in you which was also in Christ Jesus,
who, being in the form of God,
    was made in the likeness of men.
And being found in fashion as a man,
    He humbled Himself,
        and became obedient unto death,

even the death of the cross.'

Like our Lord,
　we must always
　　and only think of our identity and our destiny
　　　with humility.
Then, and only then, will we have the mind of Christ.
Then, and only then, will our thoughts be Christ's thoughts.

But—*how*?

　Paul, speaking from his own experience, in effect offers the
answer to this question in 2 Corinthians, chapter 10 and
verse 5.
'We compel,' he says, 'every human thought to surrender
in obedience to Christ.'

Turn those words over and over in your mind.
'We compel every human thought to surrender in obedience
to Christ.'
When we do that,
　we begin to possess the mind of Christ.
Then, and only then,
　do our thoughts become the thoughts of Christ.

THREE

Christian Credentials

'My deeds . . . are my credentials'   John 10 verse 25

Every now and again the translators of the *New English Bible* manage to produce a phrase which sounds just right to our twentieth-century ears. This they do in their translation of John chapter 10 and verse 25, when they make our Lord to say, 'My deeds done in my Father's name are my credentials, but because you are not sheep of my flock you do not believe.' Let's concentrate our attention on just five words in that verse. Says our Lord in reply to those who were questioning Him, who were positively challenging Him—
'My deeds . . . are my credentials.'

Our Lord's fellow Jews were saying to Him something like this. 'You glibly call God your Father, and all the time you seem to be hinting that you are the Son of God—prove it! Go on then—prove it!'

What was our Lord's reaction to this blunt challenge? Did He proudly ignore it—and suggest thereby that it wasn't worthy of His attention?

No, He didn't!

Did He then humbly confess (as many might have considered Him justified in confessing) that He was quite unable to prove His identity? After all, He hadn't been issued with a Divine birth certificate or with a celestial visa.

No, He didn't!

Instead,

looking His challengers straight in the eyes,

He said to them something like this.

'I can—and I will prove to you my identity.
        God *is* my Father—and I *am* the Son of God—
            and I can prove it.
As a matter of fact,' He triumphantly went on,
                    'My deeds . . . are my credentials.'

But when our Lord originally uttered these words, to what sort of *deeds* was He referring? Was He, for instance, referring to certain spectacularly miraculous deeds which He had performed in order to prove His divine origin and relationship? I don't believe He was.

You see, immediately following His baptism, confronted in the lonely desert by devilish temptation, He had once and for all repudiated this method of proving that He was what He knew and claimed Himself to be. No, He wouldn't impress the people by miraculously transforming stones into bread.
No, He wouldn't convince the people by spectacularly casting Himself down from the pinnacle of the Temple.
He wasn't prepared to prove that He was God's Son by a series of spectacularly miraculous deeds!

To what sort of deeds was He referring when in response to the challenge of the Jews He said,
                'My deeds . . . are my credentials'?

The Gospel passage in which our text is to be found provides us with the answer to this question. As a matter of fact, it might be said that our Lord Himself provides the answer.

A moment or so after He had responded to their challenge, the infuriated Jews reached for missiles to stone our Lord to death. Promptly our Lord stayed their malicious hands by demanding,
'I have set before you many *good deeds* . . . for which of these would you stone me?' So we may take it that our Lord's response to the challenge of His fellow Jews, to the challenge of those who insisted that He should prove His claim to be the Son of God, was this—
                'My deeds—my good deeds . . . are my credentials.'

Now we Christian people, like our Lord before us, make some pretty remarkable claims.

Indeed, just like our Lord before us,

we claim to be 'the children of God'—no less than that.

And of course, again like our Lord before us,

we are for ever being challenged, directly or indirectly,

to prove that we are what we claim to be.

Say the people of the world to us in effect,

'So you are a son—a daughter—of God, are you? Very well then—prove it.

Go on then—prove it!'

Now what should be our reaction to such a challenge as this?

Ought we rather proudly to ignore it—and suggest thereby that it's not worthy of our attention?

Certainly not!

Ought we, then, with due humility to confess that we are quite unable to prove that we are God's children? After all, no more than our Lord before us, have we been issued with Divine birth certificates or identity cards.

Should we Christians then confess in effect to those who challenge us, 'I can't prove to you that I'm a child of God. You see, it all has to do with what I *believe*—and I can't prove to you what I do or do not believe. All I can do is to tell you that I believe this, that, or the other—and you must then either "take it or leave it".'

Or, should we Christians say (as many Christians these days seem rather lamely to be saying)—'I can't prove to you that I am a child of God. You see, it all has to do with what I *feel*, and I cannot finally prove to you that I do or do not feel anything. All I can do is to report my feelings—and you must then either accept or reject my report.'

Say the people of the world to all Christians—

23

'You claim to be children of God. All right, go on and
prove it.'
Should we react and respond by saying in so many words—
'No, I won't'—or—'No, I can't'?
I don't believe so.
With all my heart I believe that
like our Lord before us,
   we *can*
      and we *must* prove beyond all possible doubt
that we are what we claim to be—
   the very children of God.
And in my judgement, the only possible way in which we
can do this is by the superior quality of our living.
In other words, to use the language of Jesus—
as Christian people,
   claiming nothing less than kinship with Almighty God—
      'our credentials . . . are our deeds—our good deeds'.

Of course, as Christian people we have certain beliefs.
Indeed, it is our beliefs that make us what as Christians we
are.
'As many as received Him, to them gave He the authority to
become the sons of God, even to them that *believe* on His
name.'
   Then too, of course, as Christian people we experience
certain feelings. Our Lord Himself once stated that He had
come in order to ensure that our '*joy* might me complete'.
But believing what we do believe, and feeling what we do
feel, it is still our actions which prove that we are what we
are.
'Our deeds . . . are our credentials.'
   In this connection an entry in Dag Hammarskjold's diary
for 1955 recently caught my attention. 'In our era, the road
to holiness necessarily passes through the world of *action*.'
And I would add—'The proof of holiness also lies in the world
of *action*.'

24

In other words, as Christian people, claiming to have entered into a unique relationship with God—
  our deeds are our only possible credentials.

But when we refer to 'deeds' being our Christian credentials, to what are we referring?
Are we for example referring to what we do *for* God in terms of public, well-publicised activity?
Are we even referring to the amount of time and energy which we loudly, or quietly, spend in and for the Church and its various organisations?
We must never underestimate all the hard, honest work which people put into the Church and its various activities, some of it seen, but much of it quite unseen and unsung. We need more, and not fewer people who are prepared to do more of such work *for* God.
In the end, however, what in such terms we do *for* God cannot be regarded as proof of our relationship with God. What we might call 'Church deeds' are not adequate Christian Credentials.
And if we have any doubts about that, we need only recall something that our Lord once said.
'Not everyone who calls me Lord, Lord, will enter the Kingdom of Heaven.'
He went on,
'When that day comes, many will say, "Lord, Lord, did we not prophesy in your name, cast out devils in your name and perform many miracles?" Then I will tell them to their face—"I never knew you—out of my sight, you and your wicked ways".'

Clearly when we refer to Christian Credentials we are not referring merely to what we do for God.

  But of course, by the same token, we are not referring to
    what we do *with* God.

We live today in a world which is a strange paradoxical combination of incredulity and credulity.

By and large the world is incredulous—indeed positively sceptical about religion in general and about Christianity in particular. No sooner, however, does some spectacular, wonder-working, miracle-performer draw attention to himself, than he is speedily furnished with a credulous following, with a whole company of people who are prepared to believe in him because of the spectacular things which in God's name he is apparently able to do.

'See', they say, 'what remarkable influence he must have with God.' 'Look', they often seem to say in effect, 'what he can do with God.'

But are spectacular deeds to be considered worthy Christian credentials—prayers spectacularly answered, miracles spectacularly performed, and so on? Certainly not! Our Lord Himself rejected the spectacular credential—and so must we.

But if when we refer to Christian credentials we are not speaking about what we do for or what we do with God— what *are* we talking about?

Put it this way : when as Christians we say that 'Good deeds are our credentials' we are really talking about

what we do W I T H *ourselves* F O R *others.*

In fact, really we're speaking about what we might just as well describe as sacrificial service—

or perhaps even more accurately, C O S T L Y C A R I N G.

In the Gospels we are told that our Lord 'went about doing good'—at immense cost to Himself. In this expensive good which He did, lay His ultimate credentials. And so it is with us.

We claim to be the children of God. Our non-Christian fellows quite rightly challenge this claim. If, however, like our Lord before us,

we sacrificially serve them

and at great personal cost care for them,
they will ultimately come to recognize our claim.
Our deeds, you see, our good deeds,
     expressed in sacrificial service and in costly caring,
          are ultimately our only credentials as Christian people.

For reasons which are not quite clear to me, I still carry
about in my wallet the National Registration Identity Card
which was issued to me away back in 1949. Perhaps I still
fear that from behind a bush one day a heavily armed soldier
will leap and insist that I produce my credentials and
positively identify myself. When I was preparing this sermon,
I decided to have a look at my old identity card with my
teenage signature on it. It's still quite clearly an identity card,
but by now, as you might expect, it's a somewhat faded and
tattered specimen.

In what sort of a condition are your Christian credentials?
Are they rather faded and tattered, or is it possible that they
have been altogether lost these many years?

Or, to put the question more directly, when last in the
name of your Lord did you do someone a bit of service which
involved you in the making of some sacrifice? When last did
you engage in a bit of costly caring on behalf of someone in
real need?

If your answer is, 'Not for a very long time' or even, 'Never'
—then no matter how strong your convictions, or intense
your emotions, or how active you are in Church, or how
many spectacular answers to prayers you can quote, you are
not doing much to make the Christian Faith credible to
those who do not share it.

You see, as with our Lord before us,
     our deeds,
     our good deeds expressed in sacrificial service and costly
          caring—these and these alone—
are our Christian Credentials.

27

FOUR

Good Companions

'Noah walked with God'   Genesis 6, verse 9

If in the course of some Bible examination—the sort of examination to which we subject our children—we are asked 'What did Noah of Old Testament time do?', most of us, without a moment's hesitation would answer, 'He built an Ark.' Surely however of far greater significance than the fact that Noah built an Ark was the fact that 'Noah—walked with God.'

I want those words to be the focus of all our thinking this morning.

In my youth I passed through a very confused period. For the life of me, I simply could not balance what I was taught at Church about 'creation' and what I was taught at school about 'evolution'. At last, however, with the help of a young theological student, I achieved a certain balance when I recognized that in poetic language the Bible simply informed me *that* God created, whereas my schoolmasters were trying to explain in scientific jargon *how* God created the world and everything and everybody in it.

The Bible tells us *that* God is the Creator.

The scientist tries to tell us *how* the creator did his work.

There is however another question that can be asked about creation, and in some ways it is the most fundamental question of all—namely, *why* did God create the world? And for pretty obvious reasons, of very special interest to us—why did God create *man*?

Allow me in very simple language to offer you a threefold

answer to this question—one that you will have no difficulty in understanding or in remembering, and one which is related to the phrase—'and Noah walked with God'.

Why did God create man?
Because He wanted someone to W A L K with Him.

God wanted—in some sense or another which is altogether beyond our comprehension—God needed a bit of company.
So He created man—
    'in His own image'.
The Genesis stories of man's creation and of man's temptation are most vividly told. In some respects, however, no part of those stories is more vivid than that in which we are informed that Adam and Eve having been tempted and having succumbed to the temptation,
    'they heard the voice of the Lord God—
        walking in the garden in the cool of the day'.
Now of course, you may be tempted lightly and hastily to dismiss this sentence as an expression of primitive, particularly naïve religion. Well, may be it is! At the same time however we should not miss what it says to us about the relationship that God intended to exist between Himself and man—
    man the crown of His creation—
        man whom He had made in His own image.
    God made man (if you'll allow me to put it like this again)
        so that He might have 'a bit of company'.
Or to use again the language of our text—
    God made man so that He might have someone to walk with.

We Christian folks greatly cherish every *promise* that God makes to be 'with' His people. Think of all the text-cards and calendars which you've seen printed with such Bible verses as these. Think of all the sermons and addresses which you've heard based on such Bible verses as these—

'The Lord thy God is with thee withersoever thou goest';
'When thou passest through the waters—I will be with thee';
'Lo, I am with you always—even unto the end of the world'
—to mention only three!

We greatly cherish every *promise* that God makes to be
'with us', for perfectly well we realize how much we need His
company.

We positively need God to walk with us all through life's
journey.

But (and this is something that especially in our moments
of elation we tend to forget)—not only does the Lord our
God promise to walk with us,

He also demands that we should walk with Him.
Apparently you see—and don't ask me to explain this for I
honestly don't even begin to understand it—

God wants and needs our company,

even as we often need and sometimes want His company.

But in practical terms someone may be demanding what
all this means. Well, putting it very simply, it means that
even when we don't feel any desire for, let alone any need
of, God's company.

yet we are under a clear obligation 'to keep company'
with Him,

for at all times God wants

and may be even needs our company.

He actually made us in His own image so that we might walk
with Him.

Now, however, we must move on to the second part of
our answer to the question—'Why did God create man?'

Because He wanted someone to T A L K with Him.
Or to express it in another way, God didn't only want
company.

He wanted a *companion*.

Just as we Christians greatly cherish all God's promises

to be with us, so we greatly cherish what we often describe as the *privilege* of prayer, our right and our ability directly at any time and in any place to speak to the Lord our God. And without any doubt prayer *is* an immense privilege.

'What a Friend we have in Jesus,
All our sins and griefs to bear!
What a privilege to carry
Everything to God in prayer!'

At the same time, however, those of us who claim to be the friends of Jesus, those of us who aspire to be God's companions,

must never overlook the *responsibility* of prayer.

Never for a moment must we overlook the fact that God made us so that we might communicate with Him and so that He might communicate with us—or more simply,

so that we might talk with Him, and He to us.

God made us because He wanted someone 'made in His own image'

—to talk with Him.

But once again someone may be demanding, in purely practical terms, what does this mean?

Well, for one thing it means that we must talk and go on talking to God, that we must pray and go on praying whether we feel like it or not. Whether or not we feel in need of prayer, or inclined to pray, we must go on praying, we must go on speaking with God.

You see, the Lord our God made us so that He might have someone to talk with.

In the experience of all of us there come times when we don't feel any urge to pray. Whether we need to or not, we just don't have any desire to pray. Just as when we are ill we sometimes 'go off' our food, so at times in life we 'go off' our prayers.

Now in such circumstances, what must we do? Give praying a bit of a rest and take a kind of prayer vacation? No—never!

For our own sake we must persevere in prayer. As a friend of mine once put it, 'When you least want to pray, that's when you most need to pray.'

But, and I hope this doesn't sound blasphemous, not only for our own sake, but also for God's sake, we must persevere in prayer.
You see, God made us so that He might have someone to talk with.

We must pray and go on praying, even when we don't feel like it. That's the first practical implication of the fact that God made us because

He wanted someone to talk with Him.
Now for the second implication, which is this—
that in praying we must learn not only to speak
but also to *listen*.

Some folk seem to have reached the conclusion that God made them in order that they might speak *to* Him. That this is so may be judged from their so-called prayers—
prayers in which they simply talk and talk and talk *to* God.

Indeed, never for a single moment do they allow God to get a word in edgeways.

In this Church we have an excellent Pastoral Care Committee, one composed mainly of women who regularly visit the homes that are associated with our Church. Now what is the main qualification of a good visitor? Is it that she should be a good talker? Well, of course the visitor must have something—if possible something interesting to say for herself. But without any shadow of a doubt the best visitor is the one who is a good listener.

And I sometimes think that this is the greatest requirement in the person who would pray well.
Of course, he must speak to God in prayer.

32

* *

But in prayer he must also,
he must especially *listen* for and to the voice of God.

We find ourselves thinking about Noah. In Genesis chapters
6, 7, 8 and 9 we read a great deal about this man Noah.
Again and again for instance we come across such a phrase
as 'And God spake unto Noah'—'And God said to Noah'.
As far as I can see, however, there is no single reference to
Noah saying anything to God.

Now no doubt Noah often did speak to the Lord his
God. Above all things, however, this man who walked closely
with God
listened to what God had to say to him.
He realized that he had been made to talk *with* and not just
to talk *to* God.
And those of us who would learn to pray, really to pray, that
is,
must also recognize this great truth.
Why did God create man?
Because He wanted someone to walk with Him
and to talk with Him.

In addition, however, He wanted someone to w o r k
with Him.

Genesis chapter 1 verse 26 is a highly significant verse.
Certainly for those who ask the question 'Why did God create
man?' it's a most significant verse. Let me remind you of it.
'And God said—let us make man in our own image after
our likeness; and let him have dominion over fish, fowl and
cattle—and over all the earth.'

God completed His creation of the world. Then, so that
the world might be cared for, He created man. Clearly
man's task was to *work with* his Maker in the maintenance of
the world that had just been created.

God made man so that he might work with Him for
the good of the world. And with the same purpose in mind

God still makes men. The tragedy is that many men fail utterly either to realize or to accept this fact.

Morris West's novel *The Shoes of the Fisherman* is all about the way in which Roman Catholics choose a new Pope. The Cardinals meet to discuss the successor to the Pope who has just died. In the course of the discussion one of them, the Syrian, says this,

'Always you search a man for the one necessary gift—the gift of co-operation with God.'

> Always you search a man for the one necessary gift—
> > the gift of co-operation with God.

In other words,

> for his ability to work with God!

For this purpose, you see, man was created.

> Now Noah, who walked with God
> > and who talked with God,
> > > also worked with God.

He certainly had the gift of co-operation with God.

God, so the story goes, had decided utterly to destroy evil from the face of the earth. But so that He might not destroy the good with the evil, He needed at least one man's co-operation.

He needed a man to work with Him. Noah turned out to be that man—*par excellence!*

And just as in Noah's day God needed men to work with Him, so He still does today.

Man was made

> and man goes on being made
> > because God wants and needs someone to work with Him.

All this is very simple. At the same time it's basic to your understanding of yourself and especially of your proper relationship with God.

Like Noah of old,

you were made to walk with God,
      to talk,
    and even to work with God.

    May you, with the strength of Jesus Christ your Lord, go forth into the coming week more adequately to fulfil God's high intention for your life.

FIVE

That's the Spirit

'... *do not deprive me of your holy spirit*'—Psalm 51, verse 11

Old Testament references to 'The Holy Spirit' are of course fewer in number and lesser in significance than New Testament references. For all that, they do exist, and it has occurred to me that in a remarkably comprehensive sense Psalm 51 might be described as a prayer for 'The gift of the Spirit'—and in particular for the gifts which the Spirit of God is able to bestow on a man.

Inevitably, then, right at the very start, we find our attention caught by the phrase which lies almost exactly half way through Psalm 51. In verse 11 (and throughout this study it is the *Jerusalem Bible* translation which is used) the Psalmist prays,
'Do not deprive me of your holy spirit.'

In this form of words,
    the Psalmist is praying
        for the gift of R I G H T E O U S N E S S .
He desperately wants to be 'holy', to be *righteous*.
So he prays for the gift of the holy spirit to be left with him and never to be taken away from him.

If, as the heading of this Psalm plainly indicates, this was a prayer uttered by David 'when the prophet Nathan came to him because he had been with Bathsheba', then the awful, almost oppressive sense of guilt which runs all the way through it makes a lot of sense.

Lustfully and ruthlessly David sinned.
Bravely and quite brilliantly
Nathan the prophet confronted David the King with the
true nature of his sinfulness. Shamefully and wholeheartedly
the king repented of his sin.
Repeatedly therefore David begs for Divine mercy and
pardon,
and especially for cleansing and purification from his past
misdeed.
But David not only earnestly regrets past unrighteousness.
He also most earnestly desires future righteousness.
So he prays that the gift of the *holy* spirit might not be taken
away from him.
'Do not deprive me of your *holy* spirit.'

Doubtless on this Whitsunday morning, there are men and
women in this congregation who during the past week have
sinned. Perhaps, like David of old, they have lustfully, or
may be ruthlessly, sinned against God and man. In the course
of worship they have increasingly felt themselves to be
confronted by their sin, and now shamefully and
wholeheartedly they would repent of it.
　But not only do they regret past unrighteousness.
　　Sincerely,
　　　even urgently,
　　　　they desire future righteousness.
From bitter experience, however, they know only too well
that the mere desire for righteousness, even the strong
determination to be righteous, is on its own not enough.
　This being so, I would urge such people, humbly, but
earnestly, to join the Psalmist in his prayer for
　the Divine gift of *holiness*,
　　for the gift of the *holy spirit*.

But in verse 10 the Psalmist prays for a 'new and constant
spirit'. In this double request, I sense the Psalmist's longing

37

for *openness* on the one hand, and *directness*
on the other.
'Put into me a *new* spirit.'
A cry for O P E N N E S S.

Isn't it curious and even positively frightening how, over
the centuries, Christian people have so frequently developed
'closed minds'
in the belief that the Christian revelation is a 'closed book'
and that the Christian Church therefore becomes some sort
of 'closed shop'.

Again and again it has been this development which has
caused Christian people to yearn for 'the good old days'
and especially to long for a recovery of 'the old spirit' which
once seemed to activate the Church in more prosperous times.
But the Spirit of God is never 'old'.
Always the Spirit of God is a '*new*' spirit,
and always He leads the people of God forwards
   to what is new,
   never back to what is 'old'.
Christian people must never develop 'closed minds',
believing that their revelation of God is a 'closed book',
allowing the Church to become a 'closed shop'.
Instead,
prayerfully,
they must seek a basic 'openness' of heart and mind,
ever expecting that
'the Lord hath yet more light and truth to break forth from
His word'—and from His world.

Was it not this very 'openness' that our Lord was seeking
to encourage in His disciples when, on the eve of His
departure from amongst them, He said,
'When He comes, who is the Spirit of Truth, He will guide
you into all truth.'
He will go on guiding you into more and more truth.
The Holy Spirit is a *new* spirit,
and when with the Psalmist we pray,

38

'Put into me a *new* spirit',
  we are really praying for *openness*.

  But when we join the Psalmist in praying for 'a constant spirit',
    we are praying for D I R E C T N E S S.
  Even amongst Christian people these days there is a considerable growth of what can only be described as 'deviousness'. There are, as there always have been, straight liars, people who no longer are particularly conscious of, let alone have any particular conscience about, the telling of bare-faced lies.
  But in some ways more serious, and certainly more wide spread these days than plain unadulterated lying, is this 'deviousness', this tendency on the part of many people— including many Christian people—to tell only half the truth, or to tell the truth in such an ambiguous way that it's almost certain to be misunderstood.
  I find myself thinking of that couplet from Tennyson—

'A lie which is all a lie may be met and fought with outright,
But a lie which is part a truth is a harder matter to fight.'

  What is it that causes people—including Christian people to be devious, instead of being direct and straight?
Surely it must be that they're filled with 'variables' and that they lack one great 'constant' in life.
Their spirits are torn
  and therefore they try to turn
    in a great variety of directions
      instead of facing and heading in only one,
        invariable,
          altogether 'constant' direction.
With the Psalmist of old, if we would be delivered from deviousness,
  and have about us the quality of directness,

we must pray for the 'constant spirit'.

But the Psalmist who prays for 'a new and constant spirit'
moves on to pray for 'a steady and willing spirit'.
In verse 12 he prays, 'Keep my spirit steady and willing.'
   Some of you may be at a loss to differentiate between the
'constant' and the 'steady spirit'. To my way of thinking,
the difference is plain enough. David's prayer for 'a constant
spirit' I interpret as a request for
   the gift of 'directness'.
His prayer for 'a steady spirit' I interpret as a request for
      the gift of E V E N N E S S,
   in particular for the gift of emotional 'evenness'.
   The Psalmist's emotional life was subject to the most
violent fluctuations. One moment he was up in the clouds,
   the next he was down in the depths.
There was almost a sort of emotional instability about the
man.
Certainly he could not be described as a 'steady' man.
I believe, however, that he longed for emotional balance,
for what I've described as *evenness*.
So he prayed,
'Lord, keep my spirit steady.'
That's a prayer which many Christian people could
profitably make their own.
   It's disturbing to discover how many Christians are subject
to the most violent emotional fluctuations,
one moment up,
   the next moment down,
one moment hot,
   the next moment cold,
one moment elated,
   the next moment depressed.
Such people suffer from almost chronic emotional instability.
And more often than not,
because they are unstable,

they tend to be unreliable,
because they are unsteady,
    they tend to be unsatisfactory in much of their Christian
    work and witness.
Such people need to pray for the gift of temperamental
evenness,
    for the gift of emotional stability.
Like the Psalmist before them, they need to pray,
            'Lord, keep my spirit steady.'

    But David went on, 'Keep my spirit willing.'
Lord, grant me the gift of R E A D I N E S S—
    readiness, that is, to do Thy will.
    When our Lord returned from His agony in Gethsemane,
only to find His disciples asleep, He graciously, by way of
excuse, said to all of them, and in particular to Peter,
'The spirit is willing but the flesh is weak.'
But you know, as far as many, too many of *us* are concerned,
even the spirit is not willing to do our Lord's will. If only
it really and truly were, we would be far more able to do
our Lord's will than generally speaking we are.
    Every Minister has to serve some people who say to him,
usually with reference to some sin of the flesh, 'I want to
stop doing this, but I just can't.' More often than not,
however, the Minister discovers that the person who speaks
like this doesn't sufficiently *want* to stop sinning. In truth
he's not ready, he's not willing, to do what he knows very
well to be the will of God.
Such people need to pray for
    the gift of *readiness* to do God's will.
'Lord, make and keep my spirit willing.'

    But in his prayer the Psalmist goes on,
            'Lord, my sacrifice is this *broken* spirit.'
Can you, in these words, see a request for
    the gift of S U B M I S S I V E N E S S,

41

an expression of the Psalmist's desire for total submission to the will of God?

I once knew a strange little man who, by quite ruthless psychological pressures, on occasions backed up by a bit of physical violence, had completely broken his wife's spirit. Without question, usually without comment, that woman always quite automatically did exactly and immediately what her sick husband ordered her to do. My heart bled for that woman. No man has the right so to break another person's spirit.

Having said that, however, I would immediately move on to suggest that the Christian only achieves his highest spiritual estate

 when before his Lord
  he is 'a broken man',
when he is utterly and always unquestioningly
  submissive to the will of God,
 wherever it may lead
  and even whatever it may cost.

On this Whitsunday morning you may be inclined to pray with the Psalmist,

  'Do not deprive me of your holy spirit',
but perhaps your greatest need is to pray,
  'Lord, my sacrifice is this broken spirit.'

SIX

The Darkest Hour

'Paul and Silas, at their prayers'   Acts, chapter 16, verse 25

Each year all the North Bristol Ministers make their way
to the lovely little Moravian Church at Brockweir, on the
banks of the River Wye, for what is called a 'Quiet Day'.
We listen to a series of lectures, and over a picnic lunch and
tea we chat and laugh. The rest of the time, however, we
maintain complete silence, so that our private meditations
and prayers might not be disturbed. Even when our paths
happen to cross during the Quiet Times, we don't offer a sign
of recognition, let alone a word of greeting. I notice indeed
that following lectures, we all tend to go off in different
directions, just so that our paths might not cross, so that we
might not infringe on, let alone interrupt, one another 'at
prayer'.

In this sermon I am proposing to take a quite contrary
course of action, suggesting indeed that we should all, as it
were, gather round two men, and actually observe them
'at their prayers'.

Acts chapter 16, verses 25–26.
'About midnight Paul and Silas, at their prayers, were
singing praises to God, and the other prisoners were listening,
when suddenly there was such a violent earthquake that the
foundations of the jail were shaken.'

The first point I would have you register about Paul and

Silas is the T I M I N G of their prayers.

Quite unjustly they had been arrested,
flogged,
and then cast into a no doubt filthy,
dark,
damp cell,
and there by slimy,
rusty fetters chained to the walls.
Enough to knock the enthusiasm for religion out of many
a man!
'What's the point of praying to a God who has allowed us
to get into this mess? Before we ever set out on today's work,
    we said our morning prayers,
        and asked God to guide and to guard us.
And just look where it's got us!
Obviously if there is a God,
    He either can't or He won't hear our prayers,
        and if He does hear them,
            then He's either unable or unwilling to answer them.
All this being so, let's give up this praying business altogether!'
    In Paul and Silas' ghastly circumstances that would have
been the immediate reaction of many. I know this, for in far
less ghastly circumstances I've seen people, I've heard
people, react just like that.
    Such a reaction against prayer never even occurred to
Paul and Silas. In fact there's everything to suggest that the
ghastlier their circumstances, the more they felt inclined,
    even impelled,
        to pray.
    And I tell you what it is that makes me say that. We are
specifically told that Paul and Silas were at their prayers
    —'about midnight'.
    The 'high security block' into which Paul and Silas were
thrust was probably a dark enough hole even at midday. But
at midnight it must have been pitch black.

44

In such grim circumstances
    and especially at the grim midnight hour,
        the majority of people would have felt particularly
        disinclined to pray.
Not so Paul and Silas.
Indeed, about midnight they apparently prayed more
fervently than before.
    Many people who suffer in any way find the night hours,
        especially the midnight hours,
            quite the most unbearable of all.
By one means or another they get through the hours of day
pretty well.
But the hours of night,
    especially those in the middle of the night,
    are another kettle of fish altogether.
Of course,
these are the loneliest hours.
But, in addition, for some deep psychological reason or
another,
they also tend to be
the lowest hours for the human spirit.
    I haven't any statistics to prove this, but in illness most
people seem to be 'at their worst' in the darkest hours which
precede the dawn. Again I haven't any statistics to prove
this, but in the course of my ministry I've come to the
conclusion that more people die during the hours of darkness
than during the hours of light.
    Not only is midnight the loneliest hour—
        to the human spirit it seems also to be the lowest hour.
Certainly it's the hour when many people,
    even praying people,
        feel least inclined to pray.
But surely, just because it is the loneliest and the lowest hour,
it's at midnight when we most need to pray.
Certainly I would suggest that it's the hour during which
we're likely to benefit most from our prayers.

Already a somewhat disappointed, disillusioned man, Lloyd George once said this, 'Your friends and your enemies—judge them in the light and you will be deceived. You can only judge them in the hours of darkness.'

It is in the 'hours of darkness'
 that you particularly need the Divine friendship,
  and when 'through prayer' you make direct contact with your Lord
   in the dark midnight hours,
    you are most likely to prove His friendship.
So, observing Paul and Silas at their prayers, I would have you note and learn from the T I M I N G of their prayers.

In addition, however, I would have you note and learn from the C O N T E N T of their prayers.

Some versions of Acts 16, verse 25, seem to suggest that Paul and Silas not only 'said prayers',
 they also 'sang praises',
  as though these were two quite distinct religious exercises.
The *New English Bible*, however, makes it clear that for Paul and Silas 'prayer' and 'praise' were but one combined religious exercise.
We are told that these two brave men—
 'at their prayers,
  were singing praises to God'.
In and through their prayers they praised the Lord their God.

Now most of us, had we found ourselves in the ominous circumstances of Paul and Silas at Philippi, even if we had prayed,
 our prayers would not have consisted of praise.
Petition—certainly.
 Confession—probably.
  Intercession—well, may be.
   But certainly not praiseful adoration and thanksgiving

'Oh God, get us out of this mess as soon as possible, please!'
'Oh God, just in case they come to lynch us in the morning,

46

please forgive our sins.'
'Oh God, listen to those poor devils in the other cells.
Probably they've been cooped up here for years. If in addition
to helping us you can do a little something for them, then
please consider it.'

Anyone of us might have prayed like that, and thought
well of ourselves for doing so in the circumstances. But not
Paul and Silas.
At midnight they prayed,
   not prayers of petition or confession,
     nor even prayers of intercession,
       but rather prayers of praiseful adoration and
       thanksgiving.
Some time ago a book was produced entitled *The Power of
Positive Thinking*. Doubtless there is considerable power in
positive rather than in purely negative thought. I would,
however, urge on you what I would call 'The Power of
Positive Praying'.
Especially when we're 'up against it', how much of our
so-called praying is grossly negative. And how much more
valuable,
   even personally beneficial it would be if only it were positive.
If only,
   instead of complaining about our difficulties
     and claiming deliverance from them,
       we praised God,
not only for what He has done
   and goes on doing,
     but for what He is!
If only
   with praise we were to thank Him
     and especially to adore Him.
The danger of negative prayer is that it tends to concentrate
attention back on ourselves and on our suffering.
The merit of positive prayer, of praiseful praying, is that it

concentrates our attention on God!

Note also what I would describe as the S I D E - E F F E C T S
of the prayers uttered by Paul and Silas.
'The other prisoners were listening.'
The other prisoners couldn't help overhearing the noisy
midnight prayers of Paul and Silas.
But not only did they hear.
With surprise,
probably with considerable interest,
they listened.
Only an hour or so before they had seen those two
unfortunates
dragged past their cells
with torn clothes and lacerated backs.
They had heard the rattle of chains
and the snap of the stocks.
They knew the foul inner prison where the two men lay.
They also knew the brutal fate that probably awaited them
in the morning.
All they expected from Paul and Silas were groans and may
be a few curses.
Instead they heard prayers and praises.
So they listened—
may be as they had never listened to anything religious
before,
they listened!
What an effect the praiseful prayers of Paul and Silas must
have had on their fellow prisoners!

Of course, these two brave Christian missionaries didn't
pray 'for effect'. They knew only too well the way in which
their Lord had rounded on the Pharisees for making a show,
a parade,
an exhibition of their piety.
They didn't pray for effect.

Even so,
    their prayers did have a remarkable effect on those who
heard them. I like to think of it as a 'side-effect'.

Of course, we must never in any circumstances pray 'for
effect'. Never must we pray for the effect which our praying
is likely to produce on our fellows, Christian or non-Christian.
Prayer is for vertical, not for horizontal communication.
By prayer we make contact with the Almighty. Never by
prayer do we ever seek to influence our fellow men and
women. That's something that we must always bear in mind.
Never must those of us who conduct worship seek to preach
through prayer. Nor must any of us seek to 'witness' through
prayer.
Our prayers,
    especially our prayer-life,
        may indeed proclaim our faith.
Always, however, we must ensure that preaching and
witnessing never become the objects, but at most
    the side-effects,
        even if it be the altogether healthy side-effects of our
        prayers.

Finally I would have you note the o u t c o m e of the
prayers of Paul and Silas.

'Ah yes,' you say, 'in direct answer to their prayers they
were delivered from their fearful incarceration, and set at
liberty to continue their good work. What a wonderful thing
prayer is! I too am a great believer in prayer!'

But wait a minute.
The outcome,
    the immediate outcome of their prayer
        was not deliverance,
            but something much nearer disaster.

In any case, as I've already pointed out, they were not
praying for deliverance.
In their prayers,
    their highly positive prayers,
        they were too busy praising God.
But even if you do insist that at some point they must have
prayed for deliverance (and certainly their fellow-Christians
outside the prison were praying for their deliverance),
    you can't say that in answer to prayer they were delivered.
        Instead they came very near to being destroyed.

We are told that 'about midnight, when Paul and Silas
were at their prayers, there was such a violent earthquake
that the foundations of the jail were shaken'. Try to
imagine what happened within that jail during that
earthquake.
Could you think of a more terrifying experience
than to be chained to the walls of a tiny locked cell,
in the midst of a violent midnight earthquake?
Yet that was the immediate outcome of the two men having
been 'at their prayers'.

Prayer,
    real prayer,
        is an extremely hazardous business.
Having engaged in it,
    the chances are that you will be shaken,
        shaken to the very foundations.
So many people 'go to prayer' in the hope that they will be
gently 'soothed'.
    Actually they're much more likely to be utterly shattered.

Of course, in the end,
the shaking which follows prayer always does a lot of good,
as it ultimately did for Paul and Silas.
But in the short-run,

it can be pretty disturbing.
   at times painfully distressing.

'Danger—men at prayer.' That is the notice which
appeared outside a certain church. But the real danger of
real prayer is to those who pray. The chances
are that they will be shaken,
   if not shattered by it,
      even if in the end the shaking is found to have been
      entirely necessary,
   and the shattering to have been
      highly beneficial.

How terribly superficial is much of our praying, and especially
much of our thinking about prayer.

   I would, however, put it to you that prayer-superficiality
is bound to be demolished when we honestly consider in
depth the Philippian prayers of Paul and Silas,
their TIMING,
   their CONTENT,
      their SIDE-EFFECTS,
         and especially their immediate OUTCOME.

SEVEN

Will Power

'I will not'   Mark, chapter 14, verse 29
'Not what I will'   Mark, chapter 14, verse 36

This Passion Sunday morning I want to remind you of
something that Peter said to his Lord, as together they made
their way *towards* the Garden of Gethsemane. And having
done that, I then want to compare Peter's words with those
of our Lord as He made His agonizing prayer *inside* the
Garden of Gethsemane.

Having secretly celebrated their first Communion together,
Jesus and His disciples
under the cloak of darkness,
set out through the gates of Jerusalem,
in the direction of the Mount of Olives.
Perhaps the disciples thought that once again they were
heading for Bethany.
That night, however, our Lord had no intention of going
that far.
His destination was the murky olive garden which He knew
so well,
the Garden of Gethsemane.

Perhaps it was as they came within the gnarled shadows of
the garden that Jesus suddenly exclaimed,
'You will all fall from your faith.'

When a little earlier in the course of the Passover and

Communion supper He had remarked to His disciples that one of them was a traitor, they had all been shocked. No doubt they were even more so by this further revelation. Apparently there was not just one traitor. There were twelve traitors in the camp.

True to character, Peter was the first to react to this startling, shocking revelation. 'Lord', he said, 'Lord, everyone else may fall away.

but I will not.'

Note those last three words. 'I will not.' And having done that, compare them with the last words of Jesus as on the Rock of Agony he prayed to His Father,
'Not what I will, but what Thou wilt.'
Peter in the Garden of Gethsemane—'I will not.'
Jesus in the Garden of Gethsemane—'Not what I will.'

Between Peter's exclamation and our Lord's prayer there's only one word of difference. Yet no words could more vividly reveal how utterly different those two men were from one another.

The first thing that strikes you when you begin to compare these words of Peter with those of our Lord is that whereas Peter's exclamation was clearly an expression of P R I D E, our Lord's prayer was
a remarkable expression of H U M I L I T Y

Clearly Peter was a cut above his fellow disciples.
Like the rest, he was just a working class peasant.
But he had a sharper mind,
and he had a bigger heart than the rest—
one is almost tempted to say, than all the rest put together !

There's no shortage of Gospel evidence to indicate that our Lord Himself recognized, on one occasion at least that He publicly recognized, the superior qualities of the disciple who has come to be known as 'The Big Fisherman'.
One way and another,

Peter really was a cut above his fellow disciples.
The trouble with Peter was that he was aware of this,
  and he was proud of it.
No harm in his being aware of it.
  But plenty of harm in his being proud of it!
On no occasion did Peter more vividly betray his pride than
when in the Garden of Gethsemane he cast a withering,
disparaging glance around his fellow disciples and arrogantly
declared,
'Everyone else may fall away, Lord, but *I will not*!'

In contrast our Lord,
    who had a lot more cause to be proud,
        He was a humble man.
He was 'meek and lowly of heart'.
He came 'not to be ministered unto, but to minister'.
But a few hours before He entered the Garden of
Gethsemane
He gave a practical expression of His humility.
Girding Himself with a towel,
    the badge of a slave,
        He took a pitcher and a basin
            and He washed His disciples' feet.
Then when He reached the Garden of Gethsemane itself
He prayed,
'Father, not what I will, but what Thou wilt.'
A moving expression of His immense humility.

But when with a little more care I look again at the
Gethsemane words of Peter and of our Lord, I also see in
Peter's exclamation
    evidence of his D E T E R M I N A T I O N ,
whereas in our Lord's prayer I find
    evidence of His willing S U B M I S S I O N .

I don't think that Peter was merely boasting when he ex-

claimed, 'I will not.' Almost certainly he was screwing up his
courage for what he had begun to recognize as supremely
difficult days ahead. With his sharper mind and bigger heart,
he was probably the first disciple to sense his Lord's impend-
ing doom. And give him his due, Peter truly wanted to stick
by his Lord, irrespective of what might lie ahead. As a
matter of fact,
he was probably resolved
    and utterly determined to do so.
So with clenched fists, he declared,
'Everyone else may fall away,
    but I will not.
Even if I must die with you,
    I will not disown you.
        I will not.'
Peter was a resolute, determined man,
    who had made up his mind
        to be loyal to his Lord
            through thick and through thin.
His Gethsemane exclamation reveals this.

In contrast, our Lord's Gethsemane prayer reveals
    not determination,
        but rather, a deep submission.
Jesus, in addressing His Father, did not say,
'I will,
    I really will be true to my vocation
        and I will not fail you.'
In the Garden, Jesus didn't try to summon up enough will
power to face what He well knew lay ahead of Him.
Instead,
He humbly submitted Himself to the Father's will
and simply He said,
Not—*not* what I will.'

What a dramatic contrast between Peter and his Lord,

and how the contrast is underlined by their Gethsemane
words.
'I will not', said Peter,
    giving expression to his pride,
        and giving evidence of his determination.
'Not what I will', said our Lord,
    giving expression of His humility,
        and giving evidence of His utter submission.

In addition to all that, however, whereas Peter's exclama-
tion in the Garden was the source of his ultimate WEAK-
NESS, our Lord's prayer was the source of His ultimate
STRENGTH.

In the end,
Peter, like all his fellow disciples,
turned out to be a weakling.
True he at least stuck to his Lord as far as the hall of
Caiaphas.
Then, when a servant girl sniggered at him,
he too collapsed in a heap of blasphemous treachery.
His exclamation,
his proud determined exclamation in the Garden of
Gethsemane was really the source of his pitiful weakness.

Pride, of course, is always a source of weakness. Invariably
at some significant point in his character, the arrogant man
who indulges in showy displays and boastful talk is weak.
Pride is always a serious flaw in any man's character, and,
in the end, often in terms of complete and total collapse of
the personality, it shows. We have a proverb which neatly
warns us of this fact. 'Pride goes before a fall.' And so it
always does!
Interestingly enough, this proverb is an almost direct
quotation from the Old Testament Book of Proverbs, where
we are warned that 'pride goeth before destruction' and

again, that 'a man's pride shall bring him low'.

In the New Testament the Apostle Paul virtually issues the same warning to his fellow Christians. 'Let him that thinketh he standeth take heed lest he fall.'

Pride,
    especially any form of spiritual pride,
      is an inevitable source of weakness.
So it proved to be in Peter's case.

How do you react to the suggestion that Peter's determination, his strongly expressed determination, was also a source of weakness?

Usually we think of determination and resolution as a sign of strength in a man's character. And sometimes it comes very near to being so. At times, however, especially in what we might describe as the realm of morality and spirituality, determination and resolution can be a source of great weakness.

This was something that Victor Gollancz the publisher had to discover for himself. All his life he tried to overcome a weakness in his personality by the exercise of sheer will power. At last, however, he was driven to this conclusion : ' . . . there are things you cannot conquer by will power . . . The attempt indeed must almost certainly make matters worse. For what is at the root of every neurosis is a morbid self feeling in one form or another; an unreal involvement with the self as a thing in isolation from its proper whole. But the use of will power means the deliberate putting out in self-consciousness of personal and self-reliant effort. '*I* will do it !' So the self becomes more fully involved. . . . The way to conquer a neurosis is not to do something, but to receive something. . . . The something to be received must be received as truth and not called in as a cure.'

Then this man, who was always a great deal nearer to the

57

Kingdom of Jesus Christ than ever he realized himself, quotes our Lord's own words, 'Seek ye first the Kingdom of Heaven and all things shall be added unto you.'

What does all this add up to but to the fact that proud determination is often a source of weakness, whereas humble submission is always a source of strength.

So it certainly proved to be as far as our Lord was concerned.
Having agonised in the Garden of Gethsemane
and thereby reached the point of completely humble sub-mission,
He had the strength to endure all the ignominy and the agony that lay before Him,
on the way to
and then actually on Calvary itself.

How do you tend to face
    the troubles and trials,
        the testings and the temptations of life?
With the proud determination that come what may you will be true
    to your church,
        your Father,
            and your Lord?
If you do, then I respect you, but I also fear for you.
You see,
    such screwed up determination,
        especially if there's a touch of pride about it,
            is a regular source of great weakness in the Christian.
As it was for Peter, so it still is in us.
    How then should you face the troubles and trials,
        the testings and the temptations of life?
Like your Lord before you,
    with humble submission to the Father's will.

'Make me a captive Lord,
And then shall I be free.
Force me to render up my sword
And I shall conquerer be.

My will is not my own
Till thou hast made it thine,
If it would reach a monarch's throne,
It must its crown resign.'

In the Garden of Gethsemane, Peter exclaimed, 'I will not.'
In the Garden of Gethsemane, Jesus prayed, 'Not what I
will.'
Let us pray,
   'My Father God, not what I will, but what Thou wilt.'

EIGHT

Come Out the Wilderness

'The Spirit sent him away into the wilderness'   Mark,
chapter 1, verse 12

Think with me now about our Lord's baptism, and even
more particularly about what happened to Him after His
baptism.

Our Lord was baptised in the River Jordan. When He
was baptised 'The Spirit like a dove descended upon Him'.
'Thereupon'—and that's the precise word used by the New
English Bible—'at once'—'forthwith'—'immediately' and
'without delay'—

'Thereupon the Spirit sent Him away into the wilderness.'

The traditional site of our Lord's baptism is at a part
of the River Jordan which flows through a very dry, thirsty,
and extremely dusty land. The day I visited it, something
very near a sand storm was blowing. The only shelter from
the stinging particles of sand was down in the steep but
shallow cleft cut by the sluggish, dirty yellow river itself.
Not the most attractive setting for a baptismal service!

But that same day I was also taken to see, this time from
afar, the traditional site of our Lord's temptations. From
amongst the excavations that have been made to rediscover
the ancient city of Jericho, the so-called 'Mount of Temptation' was pointed out—a reddish brown mushroom that rose
from an otherwise flat, baked, and altogether barren desert.
There, so I was told, our Lord spent forty hot and hungry
days, cold and lonely nights, being tempted by Satan.

As far as some people are concerned,

the very fact that Jesus, whom they most firmly believe
to have been none other than 'God with us',
could be tempted—even tempted to do wrong,
is, to say the least of it, *surprising.*

So much so indeed that some folk reject the suggestion
altogether and, in effect, reduce the temptations of our Lord
to a meaningless mime. Of course, as recorded in the New
Testament, they accept that for forty days and forty nights
He was in some sense tempted. Then, however, they go on
to add, 'But of course, being who He was, He couldn't really
have succumbed to those temptations.' But surely, those
temptations endured by our Lord at the commencement
(and I believe all through his Ministry) were real temptations. This means that He really could have succumbed to
them. Of course He didn't. But He could have!
'He was tempted'—really and truly tempted—'on all points,
like as we are, yet without sin.'
Our Lord was indeed the Son of God.
But He was also the Son of Man,
and as such He really could be
and He really was tempted to do wrong.

You find that surprising? I consider it one of the most
comforting pieces of information relayed to us through the
New Testament.
Our Lord was tempted.
In the wilderness He was tempted.

But about our Lord's wilderness temptations the Gospels
really do provide us with what, at first sight, must be to
many a piece of very *surprising* information indeed. You
see, all the Gospels are agreed that the Spirit which descended on our Lord in His baptism, *that same Spirit* led
Him away into the wilderness. It was not by 'Satan' that our
Lord was led into the wilderness. Once in the wilderness He
was tempted by Satan all right.

But it was the Spirit,
    not Satan,
        that 'sent Him into the wilderness'.

Now don't you find that a little surprising? Certainly
many of us ought to. For are not many of us convinced
that the Lord our God, Father, Son and Holy Spirit, always
leads His people by still waters
    and through green, green pastures,
    and always at last into a land flowing with milk and
honey?

Would it not be true to say that as far as many of us are
concerned we are inclined actually to test the leading of
God by the degree of pleasure and even prosperity that
comes our way?
If everything is 'going well' and we are 'feeling good',
then we casually assume that we must be 'in the will of God'.
If, however, things begin to go 'wrong' and we begin to
'feel bad',
or even a little uncomfortable and ill at ease,
then we tend to assume that somewhere we must have taken
a wrong turning
and be no longer led by the Spirit.

Even Churches are inclined to make this assumption.
One of the most impressive religious documents that I've
ever read is Bruce Kenrick's little book entitled *Come out
the Wilderness*. At least to begin with this is the story of
a young theological student who was 'baffled by a strange
discrepancy'. Religion in America was thriving. New York
had literally thousands of churches, mostly very much alive.
But the vast, densely populated district in the city, East
Harlem, had virtually been abandoned by the church.
But what had caused the churches to move out from East
Harlem and for that matter, as Kenrick puts it, 'to leap frog

through New York'? In many cases it was undoubtedly the conviction that declined congregations, and budgets too, were an indication of God's will. Apparently the ground on which they stood had lost its fertility, so they must move on to pastures new. In coming to this decision they almost certainly believed that they were being 'led by the Spirit'.

Kenrick saw things differently, and in response to what he believed was God's call, acting on what he believed to be the leading of the Spirit, he went into 'The Hell of Manhattan' and established his work in the wilderness of East Harlem.

And who can now doubt that it really was the Spirit who sent Kenrick into that wilderness?

Now if churches make such a false assumption, it must surely be an assumption, a false assumption made by many —by a majority of church members. Let it not surprise you that from time to time at least, and in some cases for a very long time indeed,

the Spirit of God
leads the people of God,
collectively and individually—
into the wilderness.
After all, did not the Spirit of God
even lead the Son of God himself
into the wilderness?

But you know, when you come to think of it there really are at least a couple of rather surprising features about our Lord being led by the Spirit into the wilderness of temptation and both of them have to do with the timing of this piece of guidance.

In the first place our Lord was led out into the wilderness,
where under great physical stress,
He endured great spiritual strain,
immediately A F T E R His baptism.
Our Lord's baptism was for Him, as it had been for many of His disciples since, a great peak of spiritual experience.

Indeed, as has happened to many Christian men and women since—so for Christ Himself, His baptism was the dramatic moment when the Spirit descended upon Him.

'*Thereupon*', says the *New English Bible,* 'the Spirit sent him away into the wilderness.' The old Authorised Version expresses it even more strongly—'*Immediately* the Spirit driveth Him into the wilderness.' Our Lord's grim wilderness experience followed right on the heels of His deep, high, intensely fruitful spiritual experience in the River Jordan.

And is this not something that has happened to pretty well every Christian man or woman at some time or another in his or her life—may be immediately following the night of baptism? Is it not something that has happened to you?

In the course of some conference or convention,
during a House Party or a retreat,
when you were baptised,
or took communion,
or simply as you read or listened to the Word of God,
you have felt remarkably uplifted in spirit,
and in your moment of uplift
heaven above was 'a softer blue' and earth around 'a sweeter green',
and for you—
something lived 'in every hue that Christless eyes have never seen'.

To your surprise, however, and also to your distress, your time of uplift has turned out to be but a moment of uplift,
and within a day,
may be just within an hour or so,
it has developed into something perilously near a depression.
Instead of staying up in the mountains,
you have speedily descended into the valleys.
Instead of being allowed to remain beside the still waters
and within the green pastures,

you've positively felt yourself being driven out
into a great wilderness—
may be into some vast wilderness of intense temptation.

But we shouldn't be surprised that nine times out of ten
this happens.
The ups and downs of life—
    even of the spiritual life—
        shouldn't be allowed to take us by surprise.

After all, even on the purely psychological level this is what
happens. Even as it's only the mentally sick person who
remains for ever depressed, so it's only the mentally sick
person who remains for ever elated. The natural healthy
man knows all about the psychological ups and downs of
life. He experiences both elation and depression, and the
more healthy in mind a man is, so the more effectively he
learns to deal with both.

Now why should the Christian be an exception to all this?
By faith he does become a child of God, but to his dying day
he never ceases to be at the same time very much a child of
man.

So we shouldn't be so surprised by the ups and downs of
life, even of the spiritual life.

But of even more significance, because it lifts us at once to
the spiritual level, is the fact that this is what happened to our
Lord before us. Our Lord's baptism was very much an 'up' in
His spiritual life. Immediately following His baptism, however. He hit one of the all time 'downs' of His spiritual
experience.
Out into the lonely,
barren waterless,
sun-baked desert,
He was led,
where enduring indescribable physical discomfort,
He also endured indescribable spiritual tension.

65

'This is the way the Master trod,
Should not His servants tread it still?'

I'm convinced that it's when Christians are surprised by
the 'downs' which so frequently follow the 'ups' of the
spiritual life that much damage is done. We should not be
so taken by surprise.
After all,
   our Lord Himself was led
     by the Spirit
       into the wilderness
         immediately *after* his baptism.

At the same time, however, take careful note of the fact
that He was so led by the Spirit immediately B E F O R E His
Ministry.

Our Lord didn't just start his Ministry in the village of
Nazareth and then gradually spread the area of His influence.
He didn't just gather some neighbours around Him, then a
congregation, and then at last present His message to a
nation. No! Following two dramatic events, our Lord's
Ministry seems to have entered at once into full flood. The
first of these dramatic events was His baptism in the Jordan.
The second was His temptation in the wilderness.
Now I want to submit to you that for His Ministry
our Lord's traumatic experience in the wilderness was no less
necessary than His exultant experience in the Jordan.
He needed the spiritual 'up' of the Jordan.
but He also needed the spiritual 'down' of the wilderness.

Have you ever considered how many men, even in
Scripture, have been led by the Spirit into the wilderness as
a preliminary to their being led by the Spirit out into some
remarkable ministry, into some outstanding piece of service
for God?

66

Before our Lord there was John the Baptist. John is described as 'a voice crying in the wilderness'. He preached and baptised at a part of the Jordan which to all intents and purposes bordered the desert. And the John who did his work on the edge of the desert,

originally came forth from the desert.

Then following our Lord there was the Apostle Paul. On the Damascus Road, and then in Damascus itself, he had his great spiritual experience. Then what did he do? At once launch forth into his great world-wide pioneering ministry? No, he didn't. As he himself puts it,

'I went off at once to Arabia'

—to the desert lands,

to the wilderness of Arabia.

Immediately prior to,

in necessary preparation for His Ministry

our Lord, like others before Him, and like others since,

was led by the Spirit

out into the wilderness.

Am I addressing some Christian man or woman who is passing through some great wilderness experience? Could it be that this experience—unsought and unwanted—

simply precedes and is simply preparing you for some great ministry,

for some greater service,

as it did your Lord before you?

NINE

Total Victory

'Sing a new song to the Lord, for he has done marvellous deeds, his right hand and holy arm have won him victory'
Psalm 98, *verse* 1.

Could you think of a better text than that for an Easter Sunday morning sermon? 'His right hand and holy arm have won him VICTORY.'

The City Centre in Glasgow, the city of my childhood and youth, is called George Square. As you might expect, that rather ugly spot with its pretentious buildings and even more pretentious statues, evokes many a memory in my mind. But one particular memory of that Square dominates all others. One night in May 1945 I walked through the excited streets of Glasgow down to the Centre. For five, six years we had lived in darkness. That night every light was lit. George Square was packed with a heaving, roaring mass of humanity. What were we celebrating? We were celebrating victory in Europe. We were celebrating with such abandon because we had come very near at times to defeat.

In 1940, Winston Churchill had spurred us on to 'Victory at all costs; victory in spite of all terror; victory however long and hard the road may be.' For, as he expressed it, 'Without victory there is no survival.' But the years which followed 1940 were not all years of victory. In the course of several we suffered many a defeat. But at last, in 1945, came victory and we were able to celebrate. At last, at long last, defeat had been turned into victory.

For Christian people Easter Sunday is a day of celebration,
the day of celebration,
the day on which they most joyously recall that their Lord,
by His resurrection from the dead
turned

DEFEAT INTO VICTORY.

On this day, above all others, we 'sing a new song to the
Lord, for he has done marvellous deeds, his right hand and
holy arm have won him victory'.

'The strife is o'er, the battle done,
The victory of life is won,
Now be the song of praise began,
Hallelujah!'

When He rose triumphant from the tomb,
    our Lord turned defeat into victory,
        total victory.

But when Christian people celebrate on Easter Sunday,
they do so, not only because their Lord once turned defeat
into victory,
    but also because He goes on turning defeat into victory.
By their Lord's resurrection from the dead,
Christian people are themselves assured of *ultimate victory.*
'O death, where is thy sting? O grave, where is thy victory?
Thanks be to God which giveth us the victory through our
Lord Jesus Christ.'
'Death, all death is now swallowed up in victory.'
    But more than that, Christian people, by their Lord's
resurrection from the dead, are assured of *immediate victory,*
victory that is, not only in the final battle against 'the last
enemy of man'—which is death, but also victory in the
relentless day-to-day battle of life.

This last week I came across a rather remarkable compliment paid to Napoleon by no less a person than the Duke of Wellington. 'I used to say of him', confessed the Iron Duke, 'that his presence on the field made the difference of 40,000 men.'

Christian people, just like non-Christian people,
    day after day have to fight
       and go on fighting
         on the battlefields of life.
But in the fierce battle of life, Christian people have a massive advantage over those who are not Christians. Simply it is that they do not fight alone. All the time,
    especially in what seem like moments of defeat,
      their risen Lord is with them
and His presence on the field makes all the difference in the world,
more often than not indeed
         turning defeat into victory.

I would like to spend more time this Easter morning talking about the way in which our Lord once turned defeat into total victory, and especially of the way in which, for His disciples, our Lord goes on turning defeat into victory, into ultimate and even into immediate victory. But this morning I feel impelled to concentrate your attention on two other 'Victory Thoughts'.

First of all I would warn you that a man can be DEFEATED BY VICTORY. What do I mean by that? The poet Dryden was probably on to this idea when he suggested that 'E'en victors are by their victories undone'. I wouldn't myself accept that victors are always 'undone' by their victories. I would however concede that they *often* are and I would certainly warn you that a man, any man, *can* be defeated by victory.

70

Now I am talking about what we often describe as 'The danger of success' and a very real danger it is, probably far more real than any danger that may accompany failure. Certainly I've known more people destroyed by success than by failure, by victory than by defeat, simply because they've allowed it to 'go to their heads'.

I sometimes wonder if this was what caused Peter to deny his Lord. On the eve of his Lord's arrest, he swore that, if necessary, he would go to prison, even to death with Jesus. And, give Peter his due, he did turn out to be that much more loyal than his fellow disciples, even if his loyalty might have been more wisely expressed. In the Garden of Gethsemane, he alone made some attempt, even if it was a pretty pathetic attempt, to defend his Lord. When all the other disciples were noisily crashing through the Gethsemane shadows in a wild effort to save their own skins, Peter, the big fisherman, pulled out a hidden sword from among his clothes and waved it about, as much to the peril of himself as of his Lord's enemies. Then too, even if it was at a safe distance, he did follow Jesus to the House of Caiaphas.

Now is it possible that by the time he got there, Peter was feeling just a little 'cocky'? In front of all his fellow disciples, Jesus had forecast that he, Peter, would turn out a traitor. But he would show them all. In a way he had already shown them! He, and he alone (apart from John), had stuck by his Lord. True, he hadn't been able to do much, and probably he wouldn't be able to do much to help, but at very least he had not scattered for cover like the rest. He certainly could not be branded a traitor. So may be it was a rather proud Peter who warmed himself by the servants' fire in the courtyard of Caiaphas the High Priest. But,

'Pride goes before a fall'
and very low Peter fell!

In a way you could say that Peter was defeated by victory.

But whatever may or may not legitimately be said about Peter, it certainly could be said that many people, even that many Christian people, are defeated by victory because they proudly allow it to 'go to their heads'.

A young fellow does well in his examinations. Instead of allowing his success to make him a bigger man, he allows it to make him a smaller man with a bigger head !

A man does well in his profession, in business, commerce, or industry. Instead of becoming a gentle man, he becomes an increasingly hard and ruthless man, particularly in his judgements and even in his treatment of those who have been less successful than he.

Then there are the Christian folk who feel that by one means or another they've made a certain amount of progress in the spiritual life, achieving what they like to describe as a new 'depth' of spirituality. Christian development, even Christian service, becomes for them a source of particular joy and they discover within themselves new resources for the better living of the Christian life.

You would think that all such Christians would be increasingly grateful, gracious, gentle people, whose one and only desire it is to assist their fellows towards the victorious life. Sad to say, however, not all of them become such. Instead, not a few of them,
so far from becoming bigger people,
become smaller people with bigger heads;
so far from becoming gentler, gracious folk,
they become hard and ruthless in the judgements
which they pass on those they consider to be less 'spiritual' than themselves.

Such proud people have been *defeated by victory,* and remember,

   pride always just precedes a fall !

But the victory-thought which I particularly want to emphasise this Easter morning is that just as a man may be defeated by victory,

so a man may be

VICTORIOUS IN DEFEAT.

In the battle against Nazi Germany we turned defeat into victory and so during May 1945 we were able to celebrate V.E. Day. But perhaps 'our finest hour' as a nation was that which immediately followed Dunkirk, when really we were victorious in defeat.

Today we celebrate Easter Sunday,

the day on which our Lord turned defeat into victory by rising from the dead.

But would anyone want to dispute the fact that our Lord's 'finest hour' was on Good Friday?

That day He was stripped of everything except His dignity,

He was robbed even of life itself,

—but not of love.

'Father,' He cried on behalf of those who hated Him and who hounded Him to death,

'Father, forgive them, for they know not what they do.'

On Easter Sunday morning Jesus turned

defeat into victory.

On Good Friday morning He was

victorious in defeat.

And like our Lord before us we too must be,

because we *can* be

victorious even in defeat.

I don't want you to leave church in a state of religious euphoria this morning, being rather airily convinced that just because you call Jesus, the risen Christ, 'Lord' you will never again know

the bitter taste of failure,

73

the sour, sickening flavour of defeat.
Believe me you will,
sooner than you expect may be—you will!

As He did for Himself on Easter Day, our Lord, for His
disciples does often turn *defeat into victory*. But often times
it is rather His will that we should be, as He Himself was on
Good Friday, *victorious in the midst of defeat*.

Laurens van der Post in his book *The Seed and the Sower*
tells of a Japanese Camp Commander who, when under sentence of death for war crimes, asked John Lawrence, one of the
prisoners whom he had treated abominably, to visit him.
Lawrence went and found the Japanese officer in considerable confusion and distress. In an effort to instil the con-
demned creature with a bit of dignity and courage,
Lawrence offered him this advice:
'You can say to yourself as I used to say to my despairing
men in prison under you: 'There is a way of winning by
losing, a way of victory in defeat which we are going to discover. Perhaps that too,' Lawrence concluded, looking into
the eyes of the man who had done him much wrong, 'must
be your way to understanding and victory now.'

How you wish,
    how indeed you have prayed that for you
        defeat might be turned into victory.
Has it ever occurred to you, however, that may be your
Lord prefers you to be *victorious in defeat*?

Remember, 'There is a way of winning by losing, a way
of victory in defeat'. Perhaps it is your Lord's will that this
should be your way to understanding and V I C T O R Y now.

74

Lasting Peace

'Peace be with you!' John, chapter 20, verse 19

In a recent interview, Mrs Golda Meier, the Prime Minister of Israel, was asked what, if ever she met him, would be her first word to President Nasser of Egypt. Without a moment's hesitation she replied, *'Shalom'*—the Hebrew word for 'Peace'. 'Peace be with you.'

Amongst the very last words which Jesus addressed to His disciples was the word, *'Shalom'*, 'Peace—peace be with you!', He said.

No sooner had Jesus been arrested
than His disciples fled for cover,
and there,
behind locked doors,
they cowered for days on end.
News filtered through to them of their Lord's trial and of its outcome, of His execution and burial.
Even then they didn't dare to come out of hiding.
Every now and again one or two of them plucked up enough courage to make a foray, bringing back food,
but especially information to the rest.
Interestingly enough, the women were more prepared to do this than the men.

So it was that very early on the Sunday morning,
three days after her Lord's execution,

Mary of Magdala,
decided to visit the tomb in which His body had been laid.
No sooner had she gone, however,
than she was back with the most surprising piece of information
possible.
'I have seen the Lord!' she insisted.
'I have seen the Lord!'

Presumably her fellow disciples just didn't believe Mary,
concluding that grief had driven her mad,
or, that in a state of hysteria,
she was 'seeing things'.
Anyway, they decided to stay in hiding
and to keep the doors of their hiding place securely locked.

So it is that in John 20, verse 19, we read the words,
'Late that Sunday evening, when the disciples were together,
behind locked doors, for fear of the Jews, Jesus stood among
them and said, "Peace be with you!" '

I would like you to realize that this Easter Sunday evening,
three days after Good Friday, the risen Christ is in this
church, saying to you, 'Peace—peace be with you!'

To His greatly troubled disciples, who still on Easter
Sunday night were in hiding, Jesus, the risen Christ, spoke
peace.
'Peace', He said to them, 'peace be with you!'
And if ever a bunch of men needed to hear a word of peace,
it was those original disciples of our Lord. Why? Well, for a
start, they were so BURDENED BY SHAME.

Cooped up together in their place of confinement,
they had plenty of time to think,
especially about the events of recent days.
A matter of hours before their Lord was arrested in the

Garden of Gethsemane,
they had all pledged to Him their life-long loyalty.
It wasn't just Peter who protested his undying allegiance to
Jesus.
They all did!
Boasted Simon Peter,
'Even if I must die with you, I will never disown you.'
And, Mark in his Gospel tells us, 'they *all* said the same'.
Yet, when the crunch came,
we are told that 'they *all* forsook Him and fled'.

As they huddled together in their cramped little hide-out,
those first disciples of Jesus couldn't even look one another
in the eye.
As they remembered what they had promised,
even pledged themselves to do,
they became increasingly guilty men,
   burdened by an appalling weight of shame.
And, of course, this being the case,
   they had no peace.

   The chances are that in such a congregation as this there
are several peaceless, guilty men and women,
who are burdened by shame
when they remember what, in one context or another,
they promised,
   even pledged themselves to do,
      and yet have failed to do.

   You once promised a friend that you would stand by him
through thick and through thin. When, however, the big
crunch came, and especially when it became clear to you that
loyalty to this friend was distinctly to your disadvantage,
you ratted on him and swiftly left him to his fate.
   At the time, of course, you were well able to rationalize
what you did. 'The whole of life is a rat-race', you said to

yourself, 'and anyway, he wasn't a particularly close friend.'
Or, 'If a man doesn't look after himself these days, then
nobody else will, and anyway, I'm bound to put the welfare
of my own family before any promise, even to a friend.'

At the time, you had a complete rationalization for the
betrayal of your friend. Since then, however, you've been
troubled by certain doubts. You've never been able to look
your one-time friend in the face. On occasions, when you've
been completely on your own, you've been well-nigh overwhelmed by a sense of guilt, bowed down by a huge burden
of shame. Once you were a man at peace with yourself, now
most certainly you are not.

Perhaps the friend in question was a husband or a wife.
In this church or in that, you promised before God and an
assembled company of guests, that you would 'love honour
and cherish' him or her, and especially that you would keep
yourself only unto him—or her—so long as you both should
live. To that, however, you have not been true.

Of course, when you broke your marriage vows, you were
full of excuses, and especially free in the apportionment of
blame, trying to make yourself out as a greatly injured party.

Nowadays, however, when you're inclined to be most
honest with yourself, you tend to see things rather differently,
recognizing that it was sheer selfishness that made you act as
you did. So it is that feelings of guilt begin to assail you,
and you find yourself to be massively burdened by shame
and so utterly robbed of peace.

Or perhaps this 'friend' to whom you've been unfaithful
is none other than Jesus Christ Himself. One Sunday night,
in this church or in that, when you came to Baptism, or to
Communion for the first time, you pledged your eternal
loyalty to Jesus Christ, your Saviour and your Lord. For a
time you were true to the promises which you made.
Gradually, however, you felt that for one reason or another
you were less and less bound by such promises. You made
them when you were still too young to understand what they

involved, and especially, of course, you made them under the stress of some great emotion which tended rather to cloud your better judgement.

Now, however, when you look back on your various acts of disloyalty towards the one whom you used to call 'Lord', you feel a bit of a heel. In fact, at times, you nowadays come very near to being overwhelmed by an awful sense of guilt and shame, and so utterly deprived of any true peace of mind.

If indeed you are such a person,
    bowed down with guilt and shame over disloyalty to,
      over the betrayal of this friend or of that,
what does the risen Christ say to you on this Easter Sunday night?
As He said on that first Easter Sunday night to His disciples, burdened as they were with shame, so He says to you,
        'Peace be with you!'
And this He says to you, as He said to them, showing His nail-pierced hand and spear-pierced side.
'He died that we might be forgiven', and it's only when we know that our disloyalty has been forgiven that we are released from our guilt and shame and filled with 'the peace that passeth understanding'.

Not only did the original disciples need to hear the word of peace from the lips of their Lord because they were burdened with shame, but also because they were
      BITTER WITH DISAPPOINTMENT.

Palm Sunday inflamed the imagination
and especially the ambitions of the first disciples.
When they saw their Master acclaimed as King,
in the capital and Holy City of Jerusalem,
a whole mass of high expectations
and even of bright, bright visions began to form in their minds.
Almost overnight they could see themselves being transformed

from peasants into princes.

Less than a week later their heady dreams lay shattered at
their feet.
Their Lord had been crowned—
but only with thorns,
and His followers who had hoped one day to be powers
in the land
were feeling like so many fugitives from justice.

Even on Easter Sunday night,
the original disciples were filled with disappointment,
perhaps even with a bit of resentment.
It really wouldn't surprise me in the least if they were
inclined to be bitter—
bitter with disappointment.

If they were then certainly they must have lacked peace.

Most men and women, as they look back on their lives
suffer from at least a modicum of disappointment. In their
youth they were filled with high hopes and great expectations.
On their school reports, may be, the teacher used to write,
'This child shows considerable promise.' In the eyes of friends
they now and again caught a glint of admiration for what
they seemed capable of doing. In their own hearts they felt
the stirrings of ambition to rise in the world. For some reason
or another, however, childhood promise was never realized,
latent capacities were never developed, youthful ambitions
were never fulfilled.

So it is that many people look back over their lives with
disappointment, all the time saying to themselves, in so many
words, 'If I had my time to live over again, I would go about
things altogether differently. If only I had known then what
I know now.'

And some people thinking like this with ever increasing

regret, and realizing that to a very great extent 'life has passed them by' are inclined to become rather bitter.

And, of course, if by any stretch of imagination they feel able to blame somebody else for their frustrated expectations, then they are inclined to become more bitter than ever. 'But for him, but for her, I might have done things, I might have gone places.' A couple of times in my life, I've heard bitter men snarl that sort of remark, one with reference to his father and one with reference to his wife.

Now, if indeed you are a disappointed person,
inclined to be bitter with disappointment,
what does the risen Christ have to say to you on this Easter
Sunday night?
As He said on that first of all Easter Sunday nights to His
disciples, bitter with disappointment as they doubtless were,
so He says to you,
　　　　　　'Peace—peace be with you!'

He goes on,
'You once had high hopes and great expectations for
your life,
but I've got higher hopes and greater expectations for
that life of yours.
You wanted to live the grand life,
but I want you to live the good life,
You wanted to be a huge success,
but I want you to be a humble servant.
You wanted to be rich,
but I want you to be righteous.'

'And what's more,' Jesus continues,
'If only you'll learn to depend on me rather than on yourself,
or for that matter on others,
then you'll become the sort of man, the sort of woman,
that I want you to be.

So, peace—peace be with you!'

Not only did the original disciples need to hear the word
of peace from the lips of their Lord because they were
   burdened with shame
     and bitter with disappointment,
       but also—perhaps especially—because they were
                  BESET BY FEAR.

We are specifically told that it was 'when the disciples
were together behind locked doors *for fear* of the Jews that
Jesus came to them, stood amongst them and said to them,
'Peace—peace be with you!'

When Jesus was arrested,
the disciples almost to a man,
lost their nerve,
and panic stricken they fled for cover.
There, shivering and shaking for fear,
they stayed for at least three whole miserable days on end.
Fearful,
and therefore, peaceless men.

And, of course, in this church tonight there are many
fearful and therefore peaceless men and women. And what
do they fear? It's probably something that lies in the future.

Perhaps you're such a person.
You fear for your future happiness,
your future health,
you fear for your future security,
for your future sanity.
You fear for your parents,
your children,
your husband,
your wife.

You're afraid of disability, disease, or death.
You're afraid of poverty, or pain, or parting.

Of one, or may be of many things, you're afraid,
terribly, almost constantly,
    beset by fear,
and therefore, utterly and agonizingly, deprived of peace.

Now, if indeed you are such a fearful and therefore
peaceless person, what does the risen Christ have to say to
you on this Easter Sunday night?
As He said to His original disciples,
so He says to you,
                'Peace—peace be with you!'

Jesus didn't suggest to His disciples that their fears were
groundless, or that what they feared most they had least
cause to fear. On the contrary, He positively warned them
that they had good cause to fear the very people who had
tortured and executed their Lord. At the hands of such
people, or their like, several of His disciples were in fact
doomed to die, and Jesus never pretended otherwise. But the
risen Christ was able to assure His fearful disciples that no
matter what befell them,
He, their Lord,
    would always be with them.
They had forsaken Him,
    but He would never forsake them.
'Lo, I am with you always.'
He might have added, 'And through everything.'
Or He might have used the language of the Old Testament
and said,
'Fear thou not, for I thy risen Lord am with thee.
Be not dismayed for I am thy God.
I will strengthen thee, yea, I will uphold thee.

Yea, I will uphold thee with the right hand of my
righteousness.'

'So, peace—peace be with you!'

I never face a congregation without being conscious that
in front of me is a great mass of human need. In particular,
I'm conscious this evening that in front of me there are
men and women, many of them, most of them, for one
reason or another, in need of peace, some of them almost
crying out for a bit of peace because they are
   burdened with shame,
      bitter with disappointment,
        and beset by fear.
To such people I simply relay the words of Jesus,
   once crucified,
      now risen,
        and here present.
'Peace—peace be with you!'

ELEVEN

A Fresh Start

(A sermon preached at a Baptismal Service on New Year Sunday)
'... *he would start afresh*'   Jeremiah 18, verse 4

About an hour's drive from the centre of Washington, the Church of the Saviour have their Retreat Centre, a place of great beauty and of even greater peace. It is most appropriately called 'Day Spring'. At 'Day Spring' a potter, Bud Wilkinson by name, works at his potter's wheel.

After I had lectured at 'The Potter's House', the name given to the restaurant run by the Church of the Saviour in Washington, they graciously gave me a communion cup and paten made by Bud on his wheel and in his kiln at 'Day Spring'. Both of them carry his mark, three crosses in a row, the centre one being somewhat raised above the other two.

As I prepared this sermon I kept the cup and paten on my desk in front of me, and several times, in the course of my preparation, I took them in my hand, just to remind me of one real live potter with whom I've had contact, and especially to keep before my mind's eye the way in which a hand-potter goes about his highly-skilled work.

This first Sunday evening in the year, at this baptismal service, I feel bound to make comment on words which occur in Jeremiah 18, verse 4, especially as they are translated in the *Jerusalem Bible*.

Jeremiah, you see, in obedience to the explicit command of God, made his way to the potter's house, and then—as I did at 'Day Spring'—he watched the potter at work. And

what was it that particularly struck Jeremiah about the potter and his work? He noticed that
'Whenever the vessel he was making came out wrong, as happens with the clay handled by potters, he would start afresh and work it into another vessel, as potters do.'

Of course, what Jeremiah saw in the potter's house spoke to him of the way in which God was likely to deal with what he calls 'The House of Israel'.
As he actually puts it—
'Then the word of the Lord came to me saying,
O House of Israel, cannot I do with you as this potter?, saith the Lord. Behold as the clay is in the potter's hand, so ye are in mine hand, O House of Israel.'

To Jeremiah then,
God was the potter
and Israel was the potter's clay.

Allow me, however, to suggest that in a very real sense we are all potters and that our allotted span of life is rather like a lump of clay out of which we have the opportunity
to make something of use,
something of value.
We're all like potters.
In front of us on an ever turning wheel,
which is time,
lies a lump of clay,
which is our lives.
We have been set to the task of producing
something of use,
something of value.
What are you making of it, this lump of clay which we call 'life'?
I fear that some would be bound in all honesty to confess—
'I'm making nothing of it.'
The hours spin into days

and the days into weeks,
the weeks into months
and the months into years,
and the years into decades—
but, really and truly,
I'm not making anything out of my life.
There's no more shape to my life tonight than there was on
the first Sunday of last year, or for that matter, on the first
Sunday of the year ten years ago. There on the relentless
turn-table of time
lies my life,
like a great shapeless,
   valueless,
      meaningless lump of clay.
I know that it's all a criminal waste when so much has been
generously given me, and when so much is quite legitimately
expected of me. But I just can't stir myself to do much about
it. The more the years go by, the less I seem even to care
about it.

Some time ago one of my sons had a slight bone operation
on his foot. After the operation he had a visit from the
hospital physiotherapist who firmly insisted that he should
move and keep on moving his foot. It was painful to move,
of course, but the physiotherapist insisted and rightly
insisted that he should move and keep on moving his foot. She
knew, you see, that if he didn't the foot might seriously,
even permanently, 'stiffen up'.

If for months, for years, you've been making nothing, or
next to nothing of your life—then beware! You may be
fast approaching the stage when you are no longer even
capable of making the required effort.
   If, then, to all intents and purposes,
     you are making nothing of your life,
       may I urge you at least to MAKE A START.

No matter how painful the effort may be,
    make a start
      on that lump of clay which is your life,
so that out of it you may
    make something of use,
      may be even something of value.

But perhaps in answer to the question, 'What are you making out of life?', you have to answer 'I'm making a thorough mess of it.'
You're not an indolent,
let alone an indifferent creature.
Indeed, recognizing what a relatively short time you have
at your disposal, understanding that at best there is a distinct limit
to the number of turns
the potter's wheel of time is likely to make,
you've been very busy indeed
on that lump of clay which is your life,
seeking,
with all the enthusiasm and ability at your disposal,
to turn out something really worthwhile,
    something which may be a source of benefit to others
      and even a source of satisfaction to yourself.
Unfortunately, however, in spite of all your efforts, it doesn't seem to have 'come off'.
As a matter of fact, when you,
at this turning point of time,
look at the vessel of your life,
you're not only disappointed with it,
you're positively ashamed of it.
The more you look at it, indeed,
the more honestly you look at it,
the more you feel bound to admit that for one reason or another,
by one means and another,

you've made a proper mess of it!
If indeed this is how you see your life on this first Sunday of
the year,
what can you possibly do about it?
Well, like the potter who discovers that the vessel on his wheel
has 'come out wrong',
you must 'start afresh'.
You must MAKE A NEW START.
If you've ever seen a potter at work, you'll know that this is
something which he quite frequently does.
Discovering that the vessel just will not take on the right
shape,
he cuts it from his wheel,
then crumples and crushes it.
Perhaps, even, on his wheel,
he bangs it and beats it
until it is reduced once again
to a mere lump of clay.
Then he 'starts afresh'—
he 'makes a new start'.
Even the best of us—and that even when we're at our best—
tend to make a 'mess of life',
an awful mess of life.
That's why there's so much extra value in a service such as
this at the beginning of a New Year. It gives us the incentive
to
'make a fresh start',
so that instead of making a mess of life,
we at least begin to make something of use,
of value,
even of beauty,
from the rough clay of our lives.
And being a Baptismal Service as well, it provides us all,
particularly those who humbly come to their baptism this
night, with an extra special opportunity to
'start afresh'

with the task of moulding the vessels of our lives aright.

In a sense then we are all potters,
with the clay of our lives
relentlessly turning round and round
on the wheel of time,
just waiting for us to make something of it.
And frankly,
many of us are making nothing of it,
    and most of us are just making a mess of it.
So it is that many of us really ought to be 'making a start',
and most of us to be 'making a fresh start'
with the whole challenging process of turning the raw
material of our lives into a useful,
    valuable,
        may be even rather beautiful vessel.

At this point, of course, we find ourselves face to face with
the question, 'How?'
After all, many of us, probably most of us, have tried
    to make something of use,
        value and beauty out of our lives.
The trouble is that try as hard as we have and as hard as we
will, we always seem to end up by making a thorough mess
of it.
We've made more 'fresh starts' than there have been
New Years in our lives, but always we seem to make a worse
and ever worse mess of things.

Supposing in that Potter's House at 'Day Spring' near
Washington, Bud Wilkinson, the potter, had invited me to
'have a go' with a lump of clay on his potter's wheel. What
do you think I would have made of it? I'd have made a
complete mess of it. Add my general artistic ineptitude to
my complete inexperience and you can be absolutely

assured that I would have made a mess of any vessel which
I might have tried to produce.

But supposing the potter had stood at the other side of
the wheel guiding my hands, even from time to time
pressing his expert fingers into my piece of clay. What do
you think the result would have been then? My guess is that
between us we might well have produced something of
limited use, if not of particular value or beauty.

I've suggested that you are the potter whose responsibility
it is to 'make something'
    out of the clay of life,
      —and so you are!
But with all your many limitations, you really are a bit of
a fool if you try to do the whole job on your own,
especially when there's always an expert potter at your side,
ready to guide your hands,
and even at times to press his own highly skilled fingers
into the clay of your life,
so that it might begin to take on a shape which might benefit
others,
    and of which you yourself need not be ashamed.
The expert potter to whom I refer is, of course, none other
than Jesus Christ,
    Son of man
      and Son of God,
        crucified and now risen,
who even at this very moment stands by your side,
so that in co-operation with yourself,
He might begin to turn a mere lump of clay
    into something of wide use,
      of real worth,
        and even of considerable beauty.
Are you now prepared to give Him that word—what we
might call 'the go-ahead'?

One final word. I suppose you could regard it as a word of warning. The longer you leave a lump of clay, and even more so the longer you work with a lump of clay,
the drier,
  the harder,
    the less malleable,
      the less pliable it becomes.
At last, indeed, I would imagine it could become so dry and so hard that even an expert potter would be able to do nothing with it. In the end he might be forced to discard it altogether.

I would strongly advise you against any further delay in
  making a start
    or in *making a fresh start*
with the moulding or the remoulding of your life.
In particular I would strongly advise you against any further delay in seeking expert,
  divine help
    in the attempt to mould or remould your life aright.
Remember,
  Jesus Christ Himself,
    the expert potter,
      is standing by,
  just waiting for a simple 'word of consent' from you.

TWELVE

Our Own Flesh and Blood

'The Word became flesh . . .' John 1, verse 14

Two heresies which still in a variety of species flourish today, have their original strong roots away back in the history of the early Church—the so-called Arian heresy which denied the true divinity of our Lord, and the so-called Docetist heresy which denied the true humanity of our Lord.

The orthodox Christian viewpoint is that Jesus of Nazareth was at *one and the same time* fully God and fully man. Not some sort of half-man and half-God, but somehow or other altogether contained within the self-same person, wholly God and wholly man. With very few exceptions, Baptists, in common with the great majority of other Christians, accept this complicated, even apparently contradictory doctrine of the person of Christ.

But for all our statements of faith, do we really and truly accept that the one who often called Himself 'The Son of Man' was altogether divine? And especially, for all our protestations of belief, do we really and truly accept that the one whom we often call 'The Son of God' was altogether human?

This second question was particularly borne in on me when recently I found myself considering the familiar statement —John 1 and verse 14—'And the Word became *flesh*'.

In John chapter 1 we have a vivid and yet somewhat obscure account of the Incarnation, of the way in which God became man. Clearly as far as this Gospel writer was concerned, Jesus of Nazareth was 'very God of very God'.

'In the beginning was the Word and the Word was with God and the Word *was* God.' But just as clearly for this Gospel writer, Jesus of Nazareth was very man of man. Indeed in an effort to emphasize this fact, he didn't merely say, 'And the Word became human'. Instead he boldly and, doubtless as far as some of his early readers were concerned, rather crudely declared, 'The Word—became *flesh*'

Having established the full divinity of our Lord, John then seeks to establish the full humanity—the complete manhood of our Lord. So, he insists, 'The Word became flesh'.

Concentrate with me for a while on John's down-to-earth description of our Lord in terms of *flesh* and notice particularly that it carries with it at least two rather staggering implications—the first of which is this: the Son of God,

who became a son of man
  must have been subject to the
LIMITATIONS OF THE FLESH.
Clearly the Apostle Paul had no doubts about this. As he put it in Philippians chapter 2,
'Christ Jesus being in the form of God,
made Himself of no reputation—(a better translation 'He emptied Himself')
—and was made in the likeness of men.
And being found in fashion as a man,
He humbled Himself
and became obedient unto death,
even the death of the cross.'

To Paul's way of thinking, the Son of God was clearly subject—and that of course, because He subjected Himself—to the limitations—even to the limitations of the flesh.

Certainly He was subject to the ultimate limitation of the flesh which we call 'death'.

Of course, it's a piece of sheer and ultimately fruitless speculation, but I am inclined to believe that had our Lord

not been crucified, then, just like any other mortal man,
He would have died. You see, 'The Word became flesh'—
and all 'flesh' is ultimately limited by death.

Rather less in the nature of speculation, I'm convinced
that all during His lifetime our Lord must have endured
His full share of suffering.
As a child, playing in His father's workshop,
He must have cut Himself at least once on one or other of
the tools that lay about.
And having cut Himself, the blood flowed,
and the finger throbbed,
and the child cried.
'The Word became flesh.'
Then too, our Lord must surely have caught at least
some of the ailments which afflicted all His fellows, both young
and old.
What childhood infections, and for that matter, what adult
indispositions confined Him to the house—
and even to His bed for days, for weeks on end?
Of course, all this we do not and we cannot know.
All we do know is that 'the Word became flesh' and that
can only mean that our Lord must have had at least His fair
share of sickness and weakness, those being the great
'limitations of the flesh'.

Of course, some people are bound to suspect, even to
reject this very 'human' picture of our Lord.

Listen to this imaginative description of Jesus produced
by the best known evangelist of our day. 'He was a real
he-man. . . . Talk about your football players. . . . He was
physically the strongest man on earth. . . . He was the most
perfectly developed man physically in the history of the
world. . . . He must have been straight, strong, big,
handsome. . . . He was no sissie.'

There was a time when that sort of rumbustious
description of our Lord would have appealed to me. Having
thought rather more deeply about the massive implications

95

of the Incarnation, however, it no longer does. Curiously
enough, I find myself nowadays much more inclined to accept
the suggestion made by a good many of the early Church
Fathers that Jesus was 'small and frail, with a long face, and
eyebrows that were joined together, dark-skinned,
red-haired'. . . . That 'He stooped'. He may even have been
something of a hunchback.

Curious how, on first hearing, that's a repulsive thought.
Yet if we really do believe that the Almighty completely
humbled Himself, even utterly humiliated Himself—
and that in order to take upon Himself 'frail human flesh'—
why should this thought repel? Ought it not rather to
attract—in so far as it reveals to us the immense lengths
to which God in His love for man is prepared to go?

'The Word became flesh'—
a statement which powerfully indicates to us that
our Lord was subject to the *limitations of the flesh*.

But surely He must also have been
subject to *temptation*—even, I would put it to you,
subject to the

TEMPTATIONS OF THE FLESH

I must confess that just as it has taken me a long time to
accept that our Lord must have been fully subject to all
the limitations of the flesh, even to rather more than those
which beset the average man, so it has taken me a long time,
even longer, to face up to the fact that our Lord must surely
have been subject to the temptations of the flesh.

Of course, verbally I've always acknowledged that our
Lord was 'tempted on all points like as we are—yet without
sin'. Always, however, there has been in my mind a sort
of 'halt sign' between what we call 'the temptations of the
spirit' and 'the temptations of the flesh'.

Of course our Lord was tempted to exercise His power

for purely selfish purposes—to satisfy His hunger for bread,
or His thirst for general approval.
He may even at times have been tempted to use unworthy
means to achieve most worthy ends.
That, after all, is what the wilderness temptations are really
all about—the so-called sins of the spirit.
But the sins of the *flesh*?
Surely the licentious thoughts that trouble every healthy
teenager never occurred to Him!
Surely there was never a single moment during His manhood
when even a remotely adulterous thought flashed into
His mind!
The temptations of the spirit—may be—
but surely never the temptations of the flesh!
But why not?
If He really was tempted '*on all points* like as we are'—why
not?
After all, we are specifically informed that 'the Word became
flesh'.
Doesn't that imply that just as
our Lord was subject to the limitations of the flesh,
so He must surely at times have been
subject to the temptations of the flesh as well?

But why spend so much time emphasizing what I've come
to believe about our Lord's limitations and temptations?
St Augustine used to say that 'The Son of God became
a son of man so that we, the sons of men, might become
the sons of God.'
In the same vein of thought might we not say that our
Lord submitted Himself to all the limitations and to all
the temptations of the flesh so that we frail creatures of time
and sense—of flesh and blood—might not have to yield
either to the temptations, or even the limitations of the flesh?

The temptations of the flesh particularly beset us all these

4—TCIY * *

days, especially those of us who are young. We live in a highly permissive society, where everything that satisfies, and especially that stimulates the flesh is not just allowed, but even positively encouraged.

Dr George McLeod, commenting on the London showing of a Swedish film which for sheer carnal crudity reached an all-time-low, had this to say: 'Paradoxically there is something satisfying about this decline. Suggestion has reached its nadir. Permissiveness has arrived in a cul-de-sac. We are animals.' And so we are!

This being so, our young people, including our young Christian people (and some not so young), are all the time beset by what we call the temptations of the flesh. So of course it's no consolation to them when we suggest—or at very least, because of our prudishness 'hint'—that the only temptations which ever beset our Lord were the temptations of the spirit!

No! Like any other youngster,
   like any other man,
      our Lord knew the full blast of physical temptation.
      Yet He did not sin.

In His victory and in His promise to be with us in our battle lie the assurance of triumph for us—even in the struggle against the sins of the flesh. He submitted Himself to such temptations so that we need not yield to them.
He also submitted Himself to the limitations of the flesh so that we might not be overcome by them.

So often we assume that our faith has everything to do with our spirits—and very little, if anything, to do with our bodies. As a result, often by way of excuse for our failure to undertake, let alone maintain, some Christian service, we say, 'Ah, the spirit's willing, but the flesh is weak. I'd love to do this, that or the other piece of Christian work, but I just haven't the strength. I haven't got the necessary stamina.'

What a far cry this from the little Apostle, tramping all

over the ancient world, carrying about with him in his
frail body the marks of human violence and the scars of
some mysterious physical disability, and yet exclaiming with
the utmost confidence,
'I can do all things through Christ which strengtheneth me!'
'Through Christ who gives the strength, I'm able, even
physically able for anything!'

Paul would never have been able to say that but for his
deep-held conviction that the Lord Christ completely
'emptied Himself'—and Himself most humbly accepted
every limitation of the flesh.

Whenever we come to the Communion Table—on which
rest the symbols of our Lord's own flesh and blood, let us
solemnly recall His words,
'Except ye eat the flesh of the Son of Man and drink His
blood, ye have no life in you'—
no life,
    no vitality,
        with which to overcome the temptations and even the
        limitations of the flesh.

THIRTEEN

The River of God

'... *the River of God*'   Psalm 65, verse 9

This past week, as never before, I was positively charmed by
the music of Psalm 65. Let's see if I can share some of my
pleasure in this 'harvest hymn' with you.
'Thou visitest the earth and waterest it,
Thou greatly enrichest it with the river of God, which is
full of water.
Thou waterest the ridges thereof abundantly,
Thou settlest the furrows thereof,
Thou makest it soft with showers,
Thou blessest the springing thereof.'

And even better—

'Thou crownest the years with Thy goodness.
The pastures are clothed with flocks,
the valleys also are covered over with corn,
they shout for joy, they also sing.'

At times, David may not have been much of a king, at
times he may not even have been much of a man, but if, as
seems likely, he produced these lines, then he certainly was
something of a poet!
As I read and re-read these lines with ever increasing
delight, I found myself thinking about a lovely little
autobiography by a certain Lyn Irvine which I came across
some time ago. In it he recounts a vivid religious experience

as described to him by an old Scottish Border woman called Peggy Gilroy. 'I was not much more than a bairn, it was Sabbath morn, and I was sitting down upon a bank. It was early in the summer time, and I was looking down upon the small flowers and wee fernies among the grass, and it came over me all at once that they were His work, my eyes were filled with tears and the thought of His love and goodness filled my heart and the joy of that day has always remained with me.'

But it wasn't just *that* quotation from Lyn Irvine's autobiography which came to mind as I read the 65th Psalm.

In particular, when I reached the 9th verse, I thought of what the sensitive Irvine as a little child did when he was first taken on holiday to the Ettrich Bridge End. Round the house he ran from the shadows and flung out his tiny hands to the hot bright sun, crying, 'I can feel Jesus! I can feel Jesus!'

In retrospect, Lyn Irvine sees this just as an expression of sheer physical delight for which he snatched the name of Christ as the only superlative in his yet very limited childhood vocabulary.

As I say, however, when I reached verse 9 of Psalm 65, I found myself thinking of Irvine's words. You see, when I read that verse, '*I* can feel Jesus'.

But what do I mean by that? Well, listen carefully to the words of that verse, and see if they don't immediately cause you to think about our Lord.

'Thou visitest the earth and waterest it;
Thou greatly enrichest it with the river of God which is full of water.'

'Thou visitest the earth.'

A perfect description of the Incarnation, when the 'Word became flesh and dwelt among us'. As a matter of fact, even in the New Testament, this is the very form of words used to describe the advent of our Lord.

He's referred to as 'the dayspring from on high who has visited us'.

Exclaimed old Zacharias the priest, with plain reference to the coming of our Lord, 'Blessed be the Lord God of Israel, for He hath visited and redeemed His people.' And the people of Nain, when they saw a dead boy raised to life again, exclaimed,

'God hath visited His people."

'Thou visitest the earth.'

The moment I saw those words, 'I felt Jesus'.

But I felt Jesus no less as I read on through the 9th verse of Psalm 65.

'Thou visitest the earth and waterest it;
Thou greatly enrichest it with the river of God which is full of water.'

How about that phrase 'the river of God' as a description of Jesus Christ, the Son of God? I don't know how you react to this suggestion, but I like it very much myself. As far as I'm concerned indeed, it provides all sorts of most helpful insights into what one often refers to as 'the work of Christ'—that is what God's Son came into God's world to do for God's people.

Now as I pointed out right at the beginning of this sermon, we're dealing this morning with poetry, with a piece of highly colourful, highly musical poetry. This being so, on this Harvest morning you'll grant me just a little bit of poetic licence when I suggest to you first of all that Jesus Christ our Lord is

A BROOK FROM WHICH WE MAY DRINK.

The Hebrews of old had a great thirst for God. The Psalmist, as was so often the case, found just the words with which to express the deep longing of his people for their God.

'As the hart panteth after the water brooks,

so my soul panteth after thee, O God.
My soul thirsteth for God, for the living God.'

And you know, Hebrews and Gentiles, men and women of ancient days or of modern times, we all to a greater or a lesser extent, share this longing, this 'thirst for God'.

St Augustine expressed it in other language, but none the less accurately when in prayer he said,
'Thou madest us for Thyself and our hearts are restless till they find their rest in Thee.'
'You made us to drink of Thee, O God, and our souls are wracked with an awful thirst until we do so.'

Of course, there are those who would insist that unlike David, or for that matter, unlike Augustine of old, modern man no longer feels this raging 'thirst for God'. I beg to differ. As a matter of fact, I would submit that the men and women of this generation, especially the young, give more evidence of this 'thirst for God' than many a generation that has gone before. What is it that causes so many intelligent young people to take such an interest in mysticism and transcendentalism? What is it that causes so many apparently pleasure-loving young people to sit at the feet of this, that, or the other money-making Guru or Maharishi? What is it that causes a couple of simple, but decent young footballers to give up their careers and become Jehovah's Witnesses?

To my way of thinking there really is no doubt about the answer to these questions.

They are panting after the Lord their God.

Their souls are thirsting for God, for the living God!

The tragedy is that so many of them are kneeling before waters that can never quench, or at least can only temporarily quench their thirst for God.

In some even more tragic cases,
they're kneeling before polluted,
poisoned waters
which are bound at last to produce a terrible sickness of soul.

But how, in these days *is* a man to quench his thirst for God? The confident words of Jesus come at once to mind. 'If any man thirst let him come unto me and drink.'
And,
'Whosoever drinketh of the water that I shall give him shall never thirst again.'

But is there any evidence to prove that those who 'come to Jesus' have their innate thirst for God truly and even permanently quenched?

All through the centuries A.D. there have been millions of men and women able with a supreme confidence to say in effect,

'I heard the voice of Jesus say:
Behold, I freely give
The living water; thirsty one,
Stoop down and drink and live!
I came to Jesus, and I drank
Of that life-giving stream;
My thirst was quenched, my soul revived,
And now I live in Him.'

Jesus Christ is a *brook from which we may drink.*

Now for a moment or two, turn with me to the no less poetic thought that Jesus Christ is
A STREAM IN WHICH WE MAY WASH.
Just as the Hebrews of old had a great thirst for God, so they had a great sense of their own 'uncleanness'. And just as they longed to quench their thirst for God,
so they longed to cleanse their souls of sin.
And once again it was the Psalmist who found just the right words with which to express the deep-set longing of his people.
'O God,' he cried,
'Wash me thoroughly from mine iniquity,

cleanse me from my sin,
for I acknowledge my transgressions and my sin is ever
before me.'

But just as there are those who would deny that modern
man has any continuing thirst for God, so there are those
who would deny that he has any continuing sense of moral
uncleanness, and therefore any continuing desire for cleansing.

Now, without question, this is only too true of a great
many people these days. They have no sense of guilt, or at
least no conscious sense of guilt.

But still there are sensitive people who feel guilty over
what they have done and still, very often, this sense of guilt
expresses itself in an almost physical sensation of
uncleanness.

I sometimes recall the young woman in my last church
who came to me in considerable distress to discuss, indeed
to confess, a moral lapse. Actually she had been more
sinned against than sinning. For all that, as she actually put
it, with an expression of self disgust on her face, 'I just feel
dirty'.

I wouldn't be in the least surprised if somebody in this
morning's service is strongly inclined to say as much, may be
even to echo the exact words of that young woman—
'I feel dirty'.

What would I say to him, what advice would I offer to
her?
Simply, ever so simply, I would urge him or her to
'come to Jesus',
    in prayer to come with humble confession to Jesus,
        being fully assured that
'if we confess our sins, He is faithful and just to forgive us
and to cleanse us—to cleanse us from all unrighteousness'.

So Jesus,
    Son of Man and Son of God,
        once crucified and now risen,

is *a brook from which we may drink,*
and also *a stream in which we may wash.*

Allow me now to share with you what is possibly the most poetic of the three thoughts suggested to me by Psalm 65 and verse 9. Certainly some of you must consider it's the most curious.

Jesus Christ is A R I V E R O N W H I C H W E M A Y S A I L.

A great many of our poets, not to mention a great many of our hymn writers, have, of course, written about 'life' as an 'ocean'. Longfellow's lines about 'ships that pass in the night and speak each other in passing' are perhaps the best known of all. You remember how they go on,

—'*So on the ocean of life we pass and speak one another,*
Only a look and a voice; then darkness again and a silence.'

But suppose for a moment, instead of speaking about 'The Ocean of Life' we talked about 'The River of Life',
and then went on to suggest that
Jesus Christ is the *River* of life,
    the only one which flows at last into the wide open sea,
        the only one which flows at last into the vast eternal
        ocean,
            which is God.

Let's develop the imagery just a little further

We all build the craft of our lives in the deep interior of some vast continent. Our urgent purpose in building is that having launched the little ship of our lives on to one of the rivers of life it will at last bear us out into the boundless eternal ocean which is God.

The trouble is that not all the rivers of life flow out into the ocean. 'Oh, but,' you say, 'what nonsense is this? Of

course, even if it is by a long tedious, meandering route, every river at last meets the sea!'
That's just where you are wrong.

I know at least one river, none other than the River Jordan, which never flows into any ocean. True it flows into a so-called 'sea'. In reality however, this 'sea' is just a completely land-locked lake, which as you very well know is actually called 'The Dead Sea'.

People are for ever saying this sort of thing to me—
'It doesn't matter what you believe, does it?
So long as a man has some sort of faith, it doesn't really matter what it is, does it?
All roads, especially all religious roads, at last lead to God, don't they?'

But if we are to take seriously what Jesus Himself had to say, it does matter what a man believes,
the content and especially the object of a man's faith does matter,
and not all roads,
not even all religious roads, do at last lead to God.
Indeed, according to our Lord,
there really is only one road which leads to God the Father.
Or to express it in the language of this morning's sermon, there's only one river
  which flows at last into the wide open eternal ocean
    which is God.
All the rest flow at last into a 'Dead Sea', into the 'Sea of Death'.

And what exactly was it that Jesus said which gives us this impression?
Here are His actual words—
'I am the way, the true way and the living way, no man, *no man* cometh unto the Father but by me.'
Jesus the way,
  the one and only true way which leads at last to God.
Jesus the River,

the river on which we may sail,
>> the only river which flows at last into the Divine Ocean.

'The River of God.'

When I see those words, and especially when I say those
words, 'I feel Jesus',
> for Jesus is the brook from which we may drink,
>> the stream in which we may wash,
>>> the river on which we may sail.
You may well remember the simple imagery of this sermon.
But far more important than that you should remember
it, is your need to do something about it—your need to
> drink, your need to wash,
>> and especially may be your need to sail on the River
>> of Life
>>> which is Christ.

FOURTEEN

The Puzzle of Life

'Now we see only puzzling reflections in a mirror . . . but then we shall see face to face' . . . 1 Corinthians 13, verse 12

In Rome there are at least two statues of the Apostle Paul. I don't know that either of them is exactly a work of art. Both of them are, however, quite massive and they certainly portray the Apostle as a most imposing figure.

One of these statues of St Paul stands, of all places in St Peter's Square, just outside the Vatican Church of St Peter. To my way of thinking, however, that statue is rather less impressive than the one which stands just outside the magnificent church which is built over the spot traditionally associated with the Apostle Paul's execution.

Driving along the Ostian Way late one evening, with the brilliant Italian sun sinking low over the River Tiber, quite suddenly and unexpectedly I came upon the Church of St Paul, its splendid westward facade of gold mosaic ablaze with the sun's last long slanting rays. Then it was that I discovered the statue, by this time with only its massive head and shoulders lit by the sinking sun.

As I looked up into this face of the Apostle, with its broad brow, deep-set eyes, acquiline nose and thick flowing beard, I thought that never before had I seen so impressive a head on any man. My eyes then wandered down the robed trunk of the statue and I thought that never before had I seen such broad shoulders or such powerful hands set on such an upright and obviously muscular frame.

Even as I looked, however, I found myself reluctantly

recalling a description of the Apostle Paul which may well go right back to the first century. 'He was a man of little stature, thin haired upon the head, crooked in the legs, of good state of body, with eyebrows joining, and nose somewhat hooked.'

Obviously in spite of the imaginative statues of him that have been created, Paul did not have a particularly prepossessing appearance—a fact incidentally which is amply confirmed by his own writings.

For all that, Paul was a most impressive *character*. May be his body wasn't all that impressive, but most certainly his mind and spirit were. Consider his words in 1 Corinthians, chapter 13 and verse 12 and see if this is not the impression which they convey. 'Now we see only puzzling reflections in a mirror, but then we shall see face to face.' Those words fully confirm my long-held conviction that whatever might have to be said about the Apostle's body, he certainly had a most impressive mind and spirit.

How do they do that? For a start, they reveal that Paul was PREPARED TO SEE THINGS AS THEY ARE.

The Apostle never saw things merely as he wanted them to be
        or even as he thought they should be.
                He saw things as they really were.
Certainly he saw himself as he was. In his own writings there is evidence that Paul had no illusions about his own appearance. In his second letter to the Corinthians he more or less concedes that as some of his critics put it, 'he had no presence'.

But Paul not only saw his physical condition as it really was. He also saw,
        and frankly confessed.
his spiritual condition as it really was.

On one occasion indeed, so shocked was he by what he saw on inspecting his own spiritual condition, that he described himself as 'the chief of sinners'.

You may, of course, be inclined to dismiss this as a piece of pretty neurotic exaggeration. To my way of thinking, however, it's infinitely preferable to the nonchalant self-deception the majority of us regularly practise.

Probably it was Paul's own reference to a 'mirror' which reminded me of the African Princess who on being presented for the first time with a mirror and having looked into it, promptly smashed it to pieces. She had always thought she was beautiful. She was just not willing to face up to the fact that she wasn't.

With regard to our moral and spiritual condition, are not many of us just like that?
We're not prepared to see ourselves as we really are,
    let alone confess it.

Like the Duchess of Buckingham, who when invited by the Countess of Huntingdon to hear George Whitefield preach, wrote,
'I thank your Ladyship for the invitation concerning the Methodist preachers; their doctrines are most repulsive, strongly tinctured with impertinence and disrespect towards their superiors in perpetually endeavouring to level all ranks and to do away with all distinctions. It is monstrous to be told that you have a heart as sinful as the common wretches that crawl on the earth. This is highly offensive and insulting, and I cannot wonder that your Ladyship should relish any sentiment so much at variance with High Rank and Good Breeding.'
Unlike the Duchess of Buckingham and unlike many of us,
    Paul saw himself as he really was.

    But the Apostle also saw life as it really was in his time and, for that matter, as it still is today.
Honestly he recognized

and confessed
that life to him was a *puzzle*.
As he expressed it, 'We only see puzzling reflections in a
mirror.'
To us, life is always
a pretty complicated and confusing,
a perplexing and extremely puzzling affair.
Life is a real puzzle.

   To make this discovery and frankly to acknowledge it is a
sign not only of honesty, but also of considerable maturity.
It's an immature man, with an undeveloped mind and very
limited experience who thinks that life is a simple affair, and
that for everything that happens in life there is a simple
explanation.

   Nothing could be farther from the truth!
Life is not a simple affair,
and for many of life's events
there is no simple, or even, for that matter,
complicated explanation.
For those who try to think deeply and widely about life
it goes on being
more and more of a puzzle,
a confusing conundrum,
and, at times,
an almost terrifying mystery.

Why should this good man,
   rather than that bad man,
this young woman,
   rather than that old woman, have to die?
I don't know!
Why, if God is a God of love,
does he allow a whole family to be buried and battered to
death in an avalanche, or hundreds of men, women and little
children to be crushed and killed in an earthquake?
I don't know!

Just as much as any of you, I find myself asking the question—'Why?' Perhaps I ask it even more frequently, for by virtue of my calling I tend to see more suffering and dying than most of you do. Time and time again I reel away from a sick-bed, from a death-bed, in confusion, completely bewildered, altogether puzzled and perplexed. Minister of the Christian Gospel though I am, much about life still deeply puzzles me. As a matter of fact, the longer I'm in the Ministry, the more puzzled, in some respects, I tend to become.

Of course there are people, Christian people, even some Christian preachers, who sound as though they had the solution to all life's problems, the answer to all life's difficulties, and with no lack of confidence they eloquently expound their ready answers. What, in all kindness, can we say about such people?

Surely only that they must be very immature, underdeveloped and especially inexperienced folk.

After all,
    even to the Apostle Paul,
        life was very much of a puzzle.

As he himself put it,
'Now we see only puzzling reflections in a mirror.'
These words reveal that Paul was prepared to see things as they really are.

They also reveal however that Paul
KNEW THAT THINGS ARE NOT ALWAYS WHAT THEY SEEM TO BE.

When you see things in a mirror you don't see them as they really are. As a matter of fact, you see them altogether round the wrong way, back to front.

Have you ever noticed that on the front of many ambulances the word 'ambulance' is spelled backwards. It's not a mistake. It's done intentionally so that drivers in their mirrors might be able at a glance to read the word the right way round. Were the word 'ambulance' printed the right way round then it would certainly be confusingly reversed in all driving mirrors.

Whenever you look in a mirror, you see everything round the wrong way, back to front.

Said the Apostle Paul, 'We see puzzling reflections in a mirror.' May we not discover in those words an indication of the fact that Paul had come to understand that things in life are not always what they seem to be?

I can well imagine that when, on his last visit to Jerusalem, Paul was arrested and then imprisoned there and in Caesarea for at least two long weary years, he must have felt bitterly frustrated. Here he was, the man whose special vocation it was to evangelise the Gentiles, whose great ambition it was to preach the Gospel in Rome at the very heart of the Gentile world, cooped up in a miserable Hebrew cell!

Then suddenly he discovered that
    the cause of his frustration
        turned out to be the means of his fulfilment.
He appealed to Caesar, and within a matter of months he was on his way to Rome, where for at least two whole years he was able in strange circumstances to fulfil his vocation and his ambition.

Note the phrase that I used a few moments ago. 'The cause of his frustration turned out to be the means of his fulfilment.'
Over the years have not many of us again and again discovered that apparent causes of frustration
    have turned out to be means of fulfilment;
even that seemingly unmitigated tragedies
    have turned out to be sources of almost unqualified blessing?

In his book *My Early Life* Winston Churchill tells how during the Boer War he was made a prisoner, a frustrating indignity which he could hardly bear. Looking back on that episode in his life, however, Churchill later felt able to write, 'This misfortune, could I have foreseen the future, was to lay the foundation of my later life . . .'

Are you now passing through a series of what seem like direst misfortunes, perhaps even of almost unmitigated tragedies? If you are then do at very least remember that
things are not always what they seem to be;
that apparent causes of frustration often turn out to be the means of fulfilment,
and that seemingly unmitigated tragedies not infrequently turn out to be unqualified blessings.
The fact of the matter is, that at best, at very best,
we only see puzzling reflections in a mirror,
and in a mirror we invariably see things the wrong way round, back to front.

Paul saw things as they really are.
He also saw that things are not always what they seem to be

But the true measure of Paul's greatness lay in his certainty that THINGS WOULD NOT FOR EVER REMAIN THE SAME.
'Now we see only puzzling reflections in a mirror—*but then,* then we shall see face to face.'
As I stood outside the lovely Church of St Paul in Rome, I tried to picture the scene on the day that the Apostle was led out to his execution.
At the end of all his travellings and sufferings,
he must surely have seemed an unimpressive little figure to the crowds that gathered to see him die.
No doubt they poked fun at him.
Probably they laughed at his crooked legs and his hooked nose.
And in all the crowd that pressed in around him as he knelt by the executioner's block,

Paul couldn't see even one friendly face.

What were his last thoughts as he bared his neck for the executioner's sword?
Well now, I've tried to depict the Apostle Paul as a *realist,* as a man who saw things as they really were.
And as such, he must surely have been puzzled. Why had God allowed such a mad sadist as Nero ever to become the Emperor of Rome? And why did God allow this evil man to torture and to butcher good Christian men, women and even their children? To that kind of question, the Apostle had no answer.

But Paul was not only a realist, he was also an *optimist,* a man who knew that things were not always what they seemed to be.
As he died, then, did Paul have in his mind the idea that perhaps his martyrdom, together with that of hundreds and thousands of his fellow Christians, would ultimately work out to the benefit of his Lord's Kingdom? If he did, then he was right, for as someone later put it, 'The blood of the martyrs was the seed of the Church.'
But surely as he looked death straight in the face, the Apostle Paul was filled not only with realism and optimism. He was also filled with unwavering confidence and the absolute certainty that neither for him, nor for any of his fellow Christians, would things long remain as they were.
Now they were puzzled and perplexed,
baffled and bewildered by their sufferings,
but *then*, then on the other side of death's valley,
they would understand what previously they had never even begun to understand; then they would be able completely to unravel what for a whole lifetime had puzzled them completely.
As then the Roman executioner's blade flashed in the sunlight, was the Apostle Paul quietly saying to himself, 'At the moment I see only puzzling reflections in a mirror,

but, thank God, soon, very soon, I shall see and I shall understand.'

'Not till the loom is silent
And the shuttles cease to fly
Will God unroll the canvas
And reveal the reason why
The dark threads are as needful
In the weaver's skilful hand
As the threads of gold and silver
In the pattern He has planned.'

FIFTEEN

Jesus—In Retreat

'Jesus . . . withdrew . . . to the hills by himself'   John 6, verse 15

When you read John chapter 6 are you not reminded of our Lord's wilderness temptations, those which followed immediately on His baptism and lasted for forty days? In particular, don't you think of the first temptation which beset Him then—the temptation to turn stones into bread?

You see, to all intents and purposes, that's what He did when on the shores of the Galilean Lake so many years ago He fed a huge multitude of hungry men and women on just five bread rolls and a couple of sardines.
True He didn't produce food for many out of nothing.
You will admit, however, that He did produce a pretty considerable quantity of food out of next to nothing!

But wait a minute, am I even hinting that when our Lord miraculously fed a Galilean crowd, He was succumbing to some temptation or another?

Indeed I'm not! When our Lord performed His miracle He did it not to meet His own need, but rather to meet the needs of others. And further, there can be no disputing the fact that His motive for meeting their need was compassion and not ambition. In feeding that hungry lakeside multitude, our Lord was succumbing to no temptation.

On the other hand, no sooner had He fed the multitude— at least so it seems to me—than He really did find Himself beset by a very real temptation, just as real as, and in some ways remarkably similar to, those which beset Him in the wildcrncss at the very outset of His Ministry.

Indeed I am convinced that just as in the parched Judaean wilderness following His baptism our Lord was tempted,

so on that verdant Galilean lakeside

following His miracle, our Lord was tempted.
As a matter of fact, I happen to believe that the lakeside temptation was really a subtle combination of two of our Lord's wilderness temptations.

The first temptation which beset our Lord in the wilderness, that to turn stones into bread, we've referred to already. In the course of the second temptation the Devil offered our Lord 'all the kingdoms of the world' in return for a single act of homage. In the third temptation the Devil invited our Lord to make a spectacle of His Divine power and so impress the credulous people of Jerusalem.

On the Galilean shores our Lord gave unmistakable evidence of His Divine power. By it the people were most certainly impressed.
So much so, indeed,
that they immediately determined there and then to 'proclaim Jesus king'.

Now I believe that this spontaneous determination on the part of the people presented our Lord with a real temptation. He knew who He was and for what He had come into the world.
King of Kings He was and into this world He had come in order to 'set up a Kingdom'.
True, His Kingdom 'was not of the world'—
but perhaps, just perhaps,
a well established 'Kingdom on earth' might in time develop into 'The Kingdom of Heaven'.

Of course, a Kingdom on earth was a good deal less than what He had set out to establish. But may be He would have to compromise and settle for second best. Or was it possible that His high and holy purpose would have to be fulfilled in lowly and even may be in somewhat unholy ways?

Many a good man both before and after our Lord has been tempted to think like that; and many a good man has succumbed to this very temptation—the temptation to think that the worthy end sometimes justifies the unworthy means.

So the determination of the people,
the quite spontaneous determination of the people to crown Him King,
presented our Lord with a very real temptation.
In the face of the temptation what did Jesus do?
Jesus, we are told in John chapter 6 and verse 15—'Jesus . . . withdrew . . . to the hills by Himself'.
In the face of temptation Jesus *withdrew*.

If you like—He *retreated*.

You might even say—He *'took flight'*.

By centuries of jingoistic politicians and historians we've been conditioned to think that in any and every battle the combatant's only intention should be to advance—or at very least and at any cost to hold his ground. Never for a single moment should he ever contemplate retreat.

But of course, as every true soldier knows, in the ruthless game of war, there are occasions and circumstances when it is not only expedient but even positively advantageous to beat a hasty retreat, to make what strategists call a 'tactical withdrawal'.

And surely in the grim battle which is relentlessly waged between good and evil, a man is often more than justified in retreating—withdrawing in the face of overwhelming odds. I would suggest that justification for doing this is to be found in the fact that the Son of God Himself, at least once, and probably more than once, did just this.

There was nothing of the ethical jingoism, nothing of the moral bravado in our Lord.

In fact,

when beset by a huge temptation,

He 'withdrew . . . to the hills . . . by Himself'.

It distresses me to hear Christian people, especially young Christian people, indulge in what I am this morning choosing to call ethical jingoism and moral bravado. And, of course, what distresses me about such people is that this jingoism almost invariably precedes moral defeat, and this bravado almost invariably precedes spiritual disaster.

I'm thinking now of the young Christian who when urged to keep away from unworthy places and forms of entertainment smiles a highly superior smile and says, 'Why? What have I got to be afraid of? If my Christian standards are not able to endure a bit of testing then they can't be up to much!'

I'm thinking now of the young, but not always young, Christian who when urged to eschew dangerous habits which often tend to escalate, confidently exclaims, 'Why should I? I feel that with strong Christian conviction such as I have, I'll be able to keep this that or the other dubious habit well under control.'

I'm thinking now of the young Christian who when he comes to the line of the hymn that exhorts him to 'shun evil companions' grins widely and says—at least to himself—'If I'm not able to hold my own in a bit of ropey company then my Christian faith can't be all that strong.'

Now such Christian people, more often than not young Christian people, I would call ethical jingoists and moral bravados!

Our Lord,

for all that He was Himself the very Son of God,

never underestimated the power of temptation.

Certainly, in the face of temptation He never indulged in bravado or jingoism.

He *withdrew*
  —He retreated
    —to the hills by Himself.
And in the face of certain temptation we do well to follow
His example.

The Apostle Paul in writing to his young converts more
than once offered this self-same advice. 'Flee fornication', he
urged. And again, 'Flee from idolatry'. And then of course,
writing to young Timothy, he exhorted him to 'Flee youthful
lusts'.

But about our Lord's 'withdrawal' in the face of temptation
we do well to note two facts.
First of all, He withdrew B Y H I M S E L F .

When beset by His temptation
our Lord could quite simply have gathered His disciples
about Him,
and with them still round about Him,
He could have gone off into the hills,
far away from the milling crowds who eagerly held out the
tempting crown towards Him.
May be, in His hour of temptation, He would have been glad
of a bit of company.
May be He would have found a certain relief in confessing
to His disciples
  —'This crown is a great temptation to me.'
May be He would have been pleased to discuss the
temptation with them—
and in His quiet humility even seek their advice.
May be, above all things, in His hour of temptation
He would have been grateful for the prayers of those who
loved Him.
In actual fact, however, He withdrew, *by Himself*—alone.

  I sometimes think that in our reaction against the
extravagancies of the Roman Catholic Church we children

of the Reformation have failed to appreciate many of the deeply felt needs of those who are sorely tempted, their need of a Confessor, their need of a Spiritual Advisor, and above all, their need of an Intercessor.

For many greatly tempted men and women there is great comfort to be found and great strength to be discovered in simply confessing the temptation to a trusted fellow Christian, in seeking his advice, and especially in being assured of his prayers.

In the last analysis however,
    the struggle against evil,
        the battle that every Christian man must ceaselessly
        wage, is a lonely one.
Everyman has to fight his own battle, by himself alone.

Our Lord recognised this. So, being greatly tempted, He 'withdrew', not only from the people, but also from His disciples. In temptation our Lord 'withdrew—by Himself'. Those of us who really know what temptation means should note this fact.

But about our Lord's withdrawal in the face of temptation we're given another piece of vital information. Not only did He withdraw 'by Himself'. He withdrew TO THE HILLS.

I suppose that with equal facility He might have withdrawn to some isolated part of the seashore, or secretly on to the flat roof-top of a friend's house. In fact, however, He retired —'to the hills'.

I can understand our Lord's retreat 'to the hills'—for high hills do something for my spirit. When I come in sight of mountains, especially, of course, the great towering, rugged peaks of my homeland, and when I find myself amongst those peaks, my spirit soars with the mountain birds, and I feel lighter, freer, stronger, clearer. Perhaps Jesus who spent all His boyhood days up amongst the Galilean hills felt a bit like that.

But His withdrawal into the hills had a far greater

significance than that. Surely as He clambered higher and
higher into the hills which border the Galilean Sea, this
man who had been almost born and bred on what we now
call the Old Testament, this man who felt Himself beset on
all sides by a devilish temptation, surely there must have
been ringing in His head those familiar lines of the Psalmist—
'I will lift up mine eyes unto the hills—
from whence cometh my help.
My help cometh from the Lord, which made heaven and
earth.'
    A moment or so ago I committed myself to the statement
that in the last analysis the struggle against evil is a lonely one,
    a battle that every man has to fight on his own—
        by himself alone.
And humanly speaking that it most certainly is!
But for every sorely tempted man there *is* 'help'—
'help' that may be obtained from none other than the Lord
God Himself—
the Eternal One 'which made heaven and earth'.
And Jesus in His temptation went up into the hills to get
this help,
for amongst the hills He felt that much closer to God His
Father.

    You who are often greatly tempted to do wrong, yet whose
great ambition it is to overcome temptation,
    you must learn to withdraw yourself.
You must 'withdraw' from tempting circumstances, or from
the people who tempt you. From time to time, indeed, you
must withdraw from all your fellows—and that to the place
where God is most real to you.
To your ever-open Church,
to the room where you say your daily prayers,
to your garden,
to some sea shore,

or may be even to some much-loved hillside.
And there in solitude and in silence—
    in deep communion with the One who made you—
        there you may obtain the help that you so deeply need.
Remember—in *His* hour of temptation Jesus withdrew . . .
by Himself . . . to the hills.